Inequality and Public Policy

This book's concern is with visible inequalities in housing, health, and education, and policy initiatives to address them.

The authors offer readers a summary of evidence on inequalities – not only in income, gender, and wealth but also in education, health, and housing. They showcase temporal and cross-country trends as well as the policy initiatives to minimize visible inequalities. The book also discusses policy initiatives and provides clarity on what works, what does not, and what may be of use when formulating public policies. Seventeen countries were chosen for focus based on their share in global population; of these, seven are given special focus, which together account for a little over half the world's population.

Offering current research as well as insights into prospects for visible inequalities, the book is an essential read for students and professionals interested in the study of visible inequalities and equal opportunity.

Bhanoji Rao is presently Governing Board Member, GITAM, and IFHE, India. He was a faculty member at the University of Singapore (1967–1978), National University of Singapore (1985–2001), and the LKY School of Public Policy (2009–2011). He served as a World Bank Economist during 1979–1985. He has authored and edited several books and monographs, as well as several journal articles.

Suresh K.G. teaches economics at the Indian Institute of Management (IIM), Bodh Gaya, Bihar, India. He holds a PhD in the area of Economics and an MPhil in the area of Management. His research articles appeared in international peer-reviewed journals like *Economic Modelling*, *Empirical Economics*, *Journal of Quantitative Economics*, and *Economic and Political Weekly*.

Pundarik Mukhopadhaya is Professor of Economics at Macquarie University, Australia. He previously served as a consultant at the ADB, World Bank, and UNESCO. His research focuses on the measurement of social welfare, economic inequality, poverty, gender disparity, and economic sustainability in developing and developed countries. He has authored 3 books and over 80 research papers in reputed journals and edited books.

Routledge Studies in the Modern World Economy

5 **The Evolution of China's Political Economy**
Rich Marino

6 **Foreign Direct Investments in Selected Emerging Asian Economies**
An Evaluation of Pandemic and Policy Shocks
Edited by Paul Cheung, Ammu George and Xuyao Zhang

7 **Linkage Power Europe**
The EU's Trade Negotiations with China (1975–2019)
Zhang Xiaotong

8 **Economic Development Parables**
From Siam to Thailand
Winai Wongsurawat

9 **The ASEAN Digital Economy**
Towards an Integrated Regional Framework
Edited by Paul Cheung and Xie Taojun

10 **The Future of Multilateralism and Globalization in the Age of the U.S.–China Rivalry**
Edited by Norbert Gaillard, Fumihito Gotoh, and Rick Michalek

11 **Nuclear Power Safety and Governance in East Asia**
Edited by Soocheol Lee, Weisheng Zhou and Kiyoshi Fujikawa

12 **Inequality and Public Policy**
Towards Visible Equality and Equal Opportunity
Bhanoji Rao, Suresh K.G. and Pundarik Mukhopadhaya

For more information about this series, please visit: www.routledge.com/Routledge-Studies-in-the-Modern-World-Economy/book-series/SE0432

Inequality and Public Policy
Towards Visible Equality and Equal Opportunity

**Bhanoji Rao, Suresh K.G.
and Pundarik Mukhopadhaya**

LONDON AND NEW YORK

First published 2024
by Routledge
4 Park Square, Milton Park, Abingdon, Oxon, OX14 4RN

and by Routledge
605 Third Avenue, New York, NY 10158

Routledge is an imprint of the Taylor & Francis Group, an informa business

© 2024 Bhanoji Rao, Suresh K.G. and Pundarik Mukhopadhaya

The right of Bhanoji Rao, Suresh K.G. and Pundarik Mukhopadhaya to
be identified as author of this work has been asserted in accordance with
sections 77 and 78 of the Copyright, Designs and Patents Act 1988.

British Library Cataloguing-in-Publication Data
A catalogue record for this book is available from the British Library

Library of Congress Cataloging-in-Publication Data
Names: Rao, Bhanoji, 1941– author. | K. G., Suresh, author. |
    Mukhopadhaya, Pundarik, author.
Title: Inequality and public policy : towards visible equality and
    equal opportunity / Bhanoji Rao, Suresh K.G. and Pundarik
    Mukhopadhaya.
Description: Abingdon, Oxon ; New York, NY : Routledge,
    2024. | Series: Routledge studies in the modern world
    economy | Includes bibliographical references.
Identifiers: LCCN 2023047565 (print) | LCCN 2023047566
    (ebook) | ISBN 9780367181284 (hardback) | ISBN
    9781032575407 (paperback) | ISBN 9780429059629 (ebook)
Subjects: LCSH: Equality—Government policy—Case studies.
Classification: LCC JC575 .R36 2024 (print) | LCC JC575
    (ebook) | DDC 323.42—dc23/eng/20231107
LC record available at https://lccn.loc.gov/2023047565
LC ebook record available at https://lccn.loc.gov/
    2023047566

ISBN: 978-0-367-18128-4 (hbk)
ISBN: 978-1-032-57540-7 (pbk)
ISBN: 978-0-429-05962-9 (ebk)

DOI: 10.4324/9780429059629

Typeset in Times New Roman
by Apex CoVantage, LLC

This work is dedicated to Bhagawan Sri Sathya Sai *the Divine in ALL Forms, recognition of which is the foundation for visibility of equality.*

Contents

Statistical Annex   *viii*

A Humble Front Note   *ix*

A Note on Data Sources   *x*

1 Introduction and Motivation   1

2 Housing   7

3 Health   16

4 Education   28

5 Women Empowerment   40

6 Hope for the Future   48

   Two Valuable Quotes   55

References   *56*

Annexes   *59*

   Annex 1 The Sustainable Development Goals 59

   Annex 2 Social and Economic Indicators Compiled by
      the United Nations, the World Bank, and IISS 60

   Annex 3 A Note on the Social Progress Index 62

   Annex 4 Income and Wealth Inequality: Trends and
      Policy Perspectives 64

   Annex 5 Adequate Housing is a Human Right 70

   Annex 6 The UN System 75

   Annex 7 Future of the UN System: Possibilities
      for Consideration 79

Statistical Annex   *82*

Index   *87*

Statistical Annex

1	Water, sanitation, and health indicators, 2022	82
2	Out-of-pocket expense and data on physicians and nurses	83
3	Incidence of tuberculosis and diabetes, 2021	83
4	Health system ranks	84
5	Countries with highest to lowest health expenditure percentage of GDP	84
6	Top 64 countries on life expectancy (LE) and rank (R)	85
7	Educational access equality and percentage with no schooling, 2022	85
8	World Economic Forum's Global Gender Gap Index: components and weights	86
9	Net Food Trade and Food Security Index	86

A Humble Front Note

As per the well-known Kuznets hypothesis, over a long period of sustained economic growth, income inequality may first rise and eventually fall. Much against the hypothesis, inequalities in income and wealth have been rising across the world, along with and despite *long* periods of economic growth.

The real contribution of Nobel Laureate Simon Kuznets should be seen in the hundreds of papers and dozens of books on income inequality written by authors from across the world. Have they contributed to inequality reduction, if not its demise? Not quite. Of what use are endless investigations into income and wealth inequalities with the twin footnotes on limitations of data and constraints on policy?

This monograph takes a different stand. It is about fine-tuning public policy to minimize visible inequalities in education, health, and housing and help promote equal opportunities.

A Note on Data Sources

https://data.worldbank.org/ is the main source of data.

Where any other source is used, due acknowledgement is given at the appropriate place.

1 Introduction and Motivation

1.1 Inequality is "Natural"

There are tall trees and short plants. There are fragrant flowers and those that look beautiful but not fragrant. There is the jumbo elephant and the queenly peacock. There is the tiny squirrel and the tinier ant. Plant and animal kingdoms demonstrate that inequalities are part of creation and are "natural".

Creation also has vast people diversity. There are whites, blacks, and browns, and of different heights and weights. Once again it would seem that inequalities are part of creation and are "natural". Do we then conclude "let us take it as it comes; let us accept inequality on all fronts, income, wealth, education, health etc."?

1.2 Equality is Human

Here is a quotable quote from the preface of *Code Name God* by Professor Mani Bhaumik:

> [W]e are intimately connected to this unimaginably vast universe, and thereby, to each other . . . What would the world be like if every man, woman, and child truly perceived that we and other beings are all cosmic kin, inseparably connected to the universal source, and through it, to each other?[1]

Humans came a long way from the practice of "survival of the fittest". Nature might condemn some as unfit to survive; but human nature does not simply condone the agony of the mother losing a child at birth or before entering age one. Research and innovation helped immensely in reducing mortality in general and infant mortality in particular. Hidden behind the improvements in life expectancy were the numerous discoverers, not only in medicine but also in transport and communication, which helped in ensuring the relatively wide distribution of medicines and vaccines as per need. Numerous rich

DOI: 10.4324/9780429059629-1

persons and families donated large sums to help the needy in terms of food aid, educational aid, and medical aid.

The recent 21st-century example of immense kindness and compassion of the global humanity was evident in tackling the COVID-19 pandemic. It started spreading from the first quarter of 2020. By early 2021, vaccines were available, and people started getting vaccinated – an exemplary accomplishment of all those involved in health sciences. There was no money count at all when decisions were made on whom to get the vaccine for and in what order. World's humanitarian spirit began to preside over all other considerations.

1.3 Public Policy Must Help

In a 2017 publication, Scheidel[2] investigates the history of inequality from the stone age to the present. A key conclusion/thesis was that historically, inequality was reduced in the wake of unpalatable events such as wars, diseases, revolutions, and state collapse. One hopes that in the 21st-century world, nations would avoid such catastrophes and yet achieve reasonably low levels of inequality via policy initiatives.

Westview Press brought out a 2018 reader on inequality edited by David Grusky and Jasmine Hill of Stanford University.[3] The collection has 74 papers organized into 9 sections dealing with theory, rising income and wealth inequality, the rich 1%, poverty, upward mobility, race and inequality, gender and inequality, how inequality spills over, and (finally) how to address the issue. *The final section occupies just 20 of the total 479 pages.* Any amount of prolonged discourse on inequality data and trends does not automatically showcase the policies that are needed and are operationally efficient.

The critical role of policy is also brought out by Alfani (2021)[4] who investigated the historical trends in wealth and income inequality over a long period (1300–2010). Here is an excerpt from the concluding statement: "*if we want a less unequal society, then we have to act to create it, as it seems unlikely that inequality will begin to decline on its own*". In this book, we go beyond the usual discourse on income and wealth inequality and focus, instead, on visible inequalities in health, education, and housing, as well as by gender.

1.4 Apropos WIR 2022

The "World Inequality Lab" brought out the World Inequality Report 2022 (WIR-2022). The Report focuses on the empirical reality on inequality in income and wealth. For instance, the income shares of the top 10% was between 40% and 60% in most regions of the world, while the wealth share of the top decile amounted to a whopping 76%. The focus of WIR being on income and wealth inequality, the suggested measures are those *such as taxing the wealthy.*

Government's role in addressing inequality is the laudable theme of the most recent book edited by Blanchard and Rodrik.[5] In addition to the editors, *30* more luminaries contributed their expertise to what one could expect as the grand finale for the policy discourse to address the problem of rising inequality.[6] The introductory statement on the publisher's website notes that the contributors were addressing: "what economic tools are most effective in reversing the rise in inequality". Taxation and public expenditure were the most discussed "tools". *There is no direct and explicit concern to monitor and address visible inequalities.*

1.5 The Laudable SDG Initiative

The 17 Sustainable Development Goals (SDGs) (see Annex 1) promoted by the United Nations to be achieved by the world by 2030 range from "no poverty" to "quality education" and from "reduced inequality" to "peace and justice". In addition to a listing of the 17 Sustainable Development Goals, the site *https://sdgs.un.org/goals* displays 169 targets. SDGs 3, 4, and 5 (good health, quality education, and gender equality) are discussed in detail in the relevant chapters following this introduction.

1.6 Indexes Galore

Ever since the launching of the first *Human Development Report 1990* by the United Nations, there has been almost a mushrooming of indicators.[7] There can be no institution better than the UN Statistical Division in regard to globally compatible and highly authentic development indicators. Similarly, the World Bank has pioneered in the collection of internationally comparable socio-economic statistics of a wide range. Annex 2 provides a bird's eye view of the indicators developed by the UN and the World Bank just to point out that the coverage of visible equality has been either nil or minimal. The Annex also explores a few more index construction attempts. While some went close to showcasing the troubles and tribulations of the less privileged, none worked out on visible equality/inequality.

1.7 The Social Progress Index

The Social Progress Index (SPI) is one of the fine attempts in the "going beyond GDP" movement. SPI is an all-encompassing measure of social progress based on social and environmental metrics. SPI was developed by the Social Progress Imperative, a non-profit organization based in Washington, DC. It was established in 2012 under the guidance of Michael Porter from the Harvard Business School and Scott Stern from MIT. Annex 3 provides more information on SPI. One can easily note that if *ALL* the implicit measures are taken to ensure social progress, there might be reduction and eventual elimination of visible inequalities; but the world is nowhere near such an enticing outcome.

1.8 Inspired by WSR 2020[8]

The World Social Report, 2020, is like a stock-taking exercise on some of the key SDGs. A few quotable quotes from the Report (pp. 13–14) are as follows:

> [T]his report highlights three building blocks of a coherent and integrated policy strategy to reduce inequality in many of its dimensions. . . . 1. Promote equal access to opportunities. . . . 2. Institute a macroeconomic policy environment conducive to reducing inequality. . . . 3. Tackle prejudice and discrimination and promote the participation of disadvantaged groups in economic, social and political life.

Towards the end, WSR (p. 150) has the magnificent idea of "an equality lens to manage mega trends" comprising the following: leverage new technologies for job creation, bridge technological divides, build resilience of people in poverty to climate change, ensure a just transition to green economies, secure urban housing and land rights for all, ensure access to basic services and public transport, expand legal migration pathways, (and) actively promote migrants' integration.

Indeed, if action is taken on all the aforementioned across all nations of the world, the need to probe into the visibility of equality would not have arisen.[9]

1.9 About This Book

Given the exceptionally vast literature, this book does not repeat the showcasing of the policy discourse on mending income and wealth inequalities, except to summarize the main findings and issues in Annex 4.

The book's concern is with visible inequalities in housing, health, and education, and policy initiatives to address them.

Housing plays the key catalytic role in ensuring healthy living and promoting educational achievements. Even today, the neighbourhoods that serve as habitats for the fairly well-to-do[10] shy away from building one/two bed-room apartments for the low-income workers (maids, security staff, and maintenance workers) and their families to live in the same neighbourhood.

In health care, money plays a pivotal role especially in developing countries. Private hospitals differ significantly compared to government hospitals in regard to facilities – both material and human.

Privatization is rampant in education. With the mushrooming of private schools for those who can afford, the first 12 years of education is serving to divide the rich and the not rich.

Rest of this book is organized as follows. Chapters 2, 3, 4, and 5 respectively deal with housing, health, education, and women empowerment – showcasing temporal and cross-country trends as well as the policy initiatives to minimize visible inequalities. Chapter 6 is on the hope for the future.

1.9.1 Countries' Selection

In the earlier paragraph, a mention was made about "showcasing temporal and cross-country trends as well as the policy initiatives". To facilitate the process, a number of countries are selected on the basis of the evidence on the demographic importance of the counters as indicated by the share in global population. World Bank population data for 1960 through 2021 updated on March 1, 2023, covers over 200 countries – China and India with a little over 1.4 billion people each in 2021 on the top and the tiny island nations – Nauru and Tuvalu at the end with 12,500 and 11,200 people, respectively. Based on the 2021 share in total global population of 7.9 billion, the top 17 countries (Table 1.1) making up for a little over two thirds (67%) are selected for general consideration in the analyses of the subsequent chapters. Out of the 17, 7 (in bold in the table), each with a minimum population size of 200 million, together accounting for a little over half the world population, will be in special focus. If these nations succeed in demonstrating visible equality in housing, education, and health care, the rest of the world will benefit via demonstration effect and assistance from friendly nations and global aid agencies.

Table 1.1 The 17 countries with two-thirds of the world population in 2021

Country	Population (million)	% of world population	Country	Population (million)	% of world population
China	**1,412**	**17.9**	Russian Fed.	143	1.8
India	**1,407**	**17.8**	Mexico	126	1.6
The United States	**331**	**4.2**	Japan	125	1.6
Indonesia	**273**	**3.5**	Ethiopia	120	1.5
Pakistan	**231**	**2.9**	The Philippines	113	1.4
Brazil	**214**	**2.7**	Egypt	109	1.4
Nigeria	**213**	**2.7**	Vietnam	97	1.2
Bangladesh	169	2.1	Congo, D.R	96	1.2
			Iran	88	1.1

Notes

1 Bhaumik, Mani (2005, 2017), *Code Name God, the Spiritual Odyssey of a Man of Science*, Penguin Random House India, p. xxviii.

2 Scheidel, Walter (2017), *The Great Leveler: Violence and the History of Inequality from Stone Age to the Twenty-First Century*, Princeton University Press.

3 Grusky, David B. and Hill, Jasmine (Eds.) (2018), *Inequality in the 21st Century, a Reader*, Westview Press.

4 Alfani, Guido (2021), "Economic Inequality in Pre-Industrial Times: Europe and Beyond", *Journal of Economic Literature*, 59(1), 3–44.

5 Blanchard, Olivier and Rodrik, Dani (Eds.) (2021), *Combating Inequality: Rethinking Government's Role*, The MIT Press, p. 312.

6 "In the United States, the wealth share of the top 1% has risen from 25% in the late 1970s to around 40% today" – from the MIT press website as in note 5.

7 A succinct discussion of the various indexes and interpretations in the Southeast Asian context is available in Booth, Anne (2019), *Living Standards in Southeast Asia, Changes Over the Long Twentieth Century, 1900–2015*, Amsterdam University Press.

8 United Nations (2020), *World Social Report 2020: Inequality in a Rapidly Changing World*, The United Nations Department of Economic and Social Affairs.

9 We have the United Nations, but the nations are not united. Perhaps, it is time that there is a relook at the UN system on the progress in accomplishing global unity in the hope that it is not a far cry, given the 2022–2023 Ukraine "war". A relatively more detailed discussion on the UN system is included in the final chapter.

10 An October 2022 advertisement about two towers (each with over 40 floors) being built in Hyderabad, India, has the "great unannounced value" of promoting visible inequality: Each floor in each tower will have only one apartment, with living area under 11,000 SFT. India being a fully vibrant democracy, there was obviously no ceiling on the floor area and no need for any regulatory approval to go for such a vast area.

2 Housing

2.1 Introduction

The emperor's gene was behind the wealth of his descendant – this could explain the prevalence of inequality over centuries, a genomic explanation along the lines of the latest (2022) work of Carles Lalueza-Fox.[1] The moment one accepts gene-induced inequality as natural and that it must be left unaddressed, it could help rationalize wealth inequality and palaces for the rich and slums for the poor.[2]

2.2 The Homeless and Slum Dwellers

The worldpopulationreview.com (accessed July 7, 2023) has a table entitled "Homelessness by Country, 2023" based on which Table 2.1 has been prepared. Homelessness is a consequence of people moving from villages and small towns (and at times even larger cities) in search of some livelihood. Most of the national capital cities and commercial capitals attract internal immigrants who settle in manual jobs and live in make-shift shelters. Some of those who are not qualified or not able-bodied might even use pavements as "shelters". Some of the homeless in due course may end up in a slum as their chosen habitat.

Based on the data on the site https://ourworldindata.org/urbanization (accessed July 5, 2023), more than 4 billion people live in urban areas globally; and close to one-in-three urban people live in a slum household. Table 2.2, derived from the data on the aforementioned site, reveals the slum challenge.

2.2.1 Housing for Overall Welfare

Proper housing is a basic need. It is a must for accessing proper water and sanitation, which in turn helps in maintaining overall health. Housing helps in promoting the feeling of inclusiveness and fostering talent when high

DOI: 10.4324/9780429059629-2

Table 2.1 Homeless and total population, 2023

Country	Homeless (million)	Population (million)	Homeless per 100 people
Nigeria	24.4	223.8	10.9
Pakistan	20.0	240.5	8.3
Indonesia	3.0	277.5	1.1
China	2.6	1425.7	0.2
India	1.8	1428.6	0.1
The United States	0.6	340	0.2
Brazil	0.2	216.4	0.1

Table 2.2 Percentage of population living in slum households, 2018

Country	%	Country	%
Brazil	16.3	India	35.2
China	24.6	Pakistan	40.1
Indonesia	30.6	Nigeria	53.9

Note: Countries covered are the six developing nations from the seven in focus

achievers in all fields live along with those who aspire and emulate. As noted by Alex Schwartz,[3]

> COVID-19 . . . reminded us of the central role of housing in sustaining public health. . . . The Trump administration was largely unsuccessful in its efforts to eliminate and curtail housing subsidy programs but did succeed in weakening programs aimed at reducing housing discrimination and segregation.

The connection between housing and health has been well explored in a special issue of the *International Journal of Housing Policy*. Guest editors for the issue were Emma Baker and Rebecca Bentley. Here is a quotable quote from the editorial:

> This collection shines a light on the potential for inequities to be manifested in, and amplified by, housing. It reminds us of the pragmatic challenges of bringing housing and health policy together, but also of the benefits of doing so. Taken together, the papers reinforce the degree to which housing affects health in a myriad of intertwined ways. Housing is a long established and central determinant of health.[4]

2.3 Ground Reality: Three Capital Cities

Regardless of a nation's per capita income and other parameters, one would generally expect the capital city to be relatively better off in housing provision and related facilities. Capital cities are homes for presidents, prime ministers, cabinet ministers, ambassadors from other countries, and so on. *The hypothetical expectation is that capital cities showcase inclusiveness and visible equality.* What is the ground reality? Rest of this section is an attempt to showcase the housing situation in the capital cities of a few of the nations in focus, starting with the US capital city of Washington DC.

2.3.1 Washington DC

The site *dcist.com*[5] has the latest on homelessness in the capital of the nation, which is globally known for its wealth and prosperity. According to the annual report released by the region's Council of Governments in early May 2023, Washington DC metro region experienced an 18% increase in homelessness between January 2022 and January 2023.[6] The increase from 7,605 to 8,944 people experiencing homelessness has been shared by all the jurisdictions, though not to the same extent. There are about 7 unhoused people for every 1,000 residents, with the underlying cause noted as a lack of affordable and available permanent housing for lower-income households.[7]

The site www.census.gov/quickfacts/DC (accessed June 25, 2023) has the estimated population of DC area: 671,083 as on July 1, 2022, with 46% white and 45% black (or African American). The situation regarding the eight wards is captured in Table 2.3: wards 2 and 3 have white majority, while wards 7 and 8 are almost wholly housing the black population.

Going by the descriptions of the wards on the DC Gov's Office of Planning site, there is no obvious explanations for the white and black concentrations respectively in wards 2–3 and 7–8. At the minimum, it can be noted that the four wards stand testimony to the lack of any "affirmative action" to promote visible equality (just to note, Ward 1 hosts the White House).

Table 2.3 Population by colour in the Washington DC wards

Ward no.	White	Black	Comment
1	44%	26%	
2	66%	8%	White domination
3	70%	9%	White domination
4	25%	49%	
5	23%	62%	
6	56%	26%	
7	3%	91%	Black domination
8	5%	88%	Black domination

2.3.2 *Beijing*

As shown in Annex 4, China has the unique distinction of having an income Gini of a little over 0.5 in 2020. Over the past four/five decades, China has rapidly evolved into a capitalist economy, of course, with communist political and governance rules.

That capitalist evolution is most widely seen in wealth inequality, manifest in visible inequality in housing. The process has been characterized as being the move from welfare-based to market-based housing allocation: "92.9% of urban residents aged 25–69 owned house property . . . in 2017, of which 39.6% purchased it from the market . . ., 8.3% purchased affordable housing . . . and 45% had self-built houses".[8] In sharp contrast, in 1988, only 13.7% of urban residents aged 25–69 owned house property, while 84.5% lived in public housing. From the turn of the century, welfare housing allocation declined/ended; home ownership rose.[9]

Current situation is rather different. "Residents Protest as China Demolishes Some of Beijing's Wealthy Suburbs" was the article posted on January 26, 2021, on www.npr.org (accessed June 30, 2023).

It has been documented that the Chinese billionaires' first choice for residence is Beijing, and then only come Shenzhen and Shanghai.[10] A 2017 article in Caixin Global has the most revealing title: Rich and Poor Are Neighbours – but Divided by Walls, penned by Wang Jing et al.[11] The core point of the article is reflected in the following (sample) statement about mixed communities:

> [O]rdinary buildings that the government requires developers to build as public rental houses or affordable homes for low-income families. . . . On the other side are commercially developed villas and condominiums for the rich, which are often set off by a towering wall.

The site www.npr.org (accessed July 5, 2023) has an audio clip titled "Residents Protest as China Demolishes Some of Beijing's Wealthy Suburbs", published on January 26, 2021. The NPR story was about the Xiangtang villa community, home for some 3,000 families. It is one of over 100 complexes selected for demolition.

Here is what an affected resident pointed out:

> Some 30 years ago, Beijing permitted the rural land to be developed into villas. They wanted to attract wealthy urban dwellers and their money to Beijing's poor suburbs. And it worked. Xiangtang became one of the best-known villages. . . . Then in October, the same government posted the notices.

From the evidence publicly available, it is difficult to conclude that the Chinese Communist Party and its leadership are promoting visible equality in housing in Beijing and allied metropolitan areas. One major problem is the enormous increase in real estate prices in the large cities like Beijing. "Since

1998 average real estate prices in China have seen a fourfold increase, while the prices in the four first-tier cities – Beijing, Shanghai, Guangzhou, and Shenzhen – have risen more than tenfold".[12]

What should be the course of action?

One area that needs reform urgently is land allocation across Chinese cities. Land supply for real estate development needs to be allocated based on actual population flows, not some man-made population targets. Development of rental markets should be encouraged and those who rent should be able to enjoy the same rights and access to public services as those who own.[13]

One must not ignore the accomplishments[14]: 86.3% of households have own housing; 96.6% have piped water at home; 98.9% have water flushing sanitary toilets; and 79% enjoy piped natural gas for cooking, while 19% use bottled LPG.

2.3.3 New Delhi – National Capital Territory (NCT)

Jones Lang LaSalle Incorporated (well known as JLL) published a commentary entitled "Surging land acquisitions in Delhi NCR".[15] NCR is NCT plus several other districts from neighbouring states. They include Gurugram, Faridabad, Rohtak, Sonipat, Panipat, Gautam Buddha Nagar, Ghaziabad, and a few more. From the core area of NCT, NCR developed via horizontal expansion. By the turn of the century, Gurgaon and Noida were leading the housing market. From around 2013, liberalized height restrictions helped the growth of high-rise buildings. Several suburbs have been gaining attention.

Data for the second half of 2018[16] (based on the National Sample Survey) shows that in Delhi NCT, 76.0% of households were using in-dwelling piped water; 71.0% households used flush/pour-flush to piped sewer system, followed by 28.5% using flush/pour-flush to septic tanks; 69.5% households were having dwelling unit owned by them; and 54% households had independent house, followed by 38.3% flats and 7.8% other type of dwelling units.

Table 2.4 Percentage of households with exclusive use of piped water by caste and religion

Caste	%	Religion	%
Scheduled Caste	70	Hinduism	76
Scheduled Tribe	63 *(lowest)*	Islam	71
Other Backward	73	Christianity	92 *(highest)*
Others	82 *(highest)*	Sikhism	90
		Others	55 *(lowest)*
Total	76	Total	76

Table 2.5 Percentage of households with tap water within premises, 2019

NCT region	Percentage	NCT region	Percentage
Northwest	84.7	West	72.8
North	56.6	Southwest	77.9
Northeast	61.7	South	56.8
East	82.5	Shahdara	*90.4 (highest)*
New Delhi	67.8	Southeast	*37.7 (lowest)*
Central	84.4	**Total**	71.0

Note: Italics font represent the max and min values

Data are also available from an exclusive "census-like survey" effort of the Delhi government.[17] It is a laudable effort since the survey was based on a door-to-door coverage of about 2 million usual residents of NCT. The data refer to the year 2019 in a broad sense.[18] As per this data, 71% of households have tap water within premises – a bit lower than the 2018 estimate. In 2019, latrine facility within premises was available to 93.34% households. "Piped sewer system is available to maximum households (60.12%), followed by 36.67% households having Septic tank arrangement of Sewer system, still 1.19% of the households in Delhi are using Flush/Pour Flush linked to Open Drain/Open Area".[19]

Clearly, there is the persistence of visible inequality from all the available evidence. From https://towardfreedom.org/ (accessed July 11, 2023), given next is an excerpt from a report of March 31, 2023, titled "India Makes Way for G20 Summit by Displacing Homeless People".

After having travelled more than 650 miles from his home city of Patna, (Rohit) Sharma lived for the past four years in a shelter the Delhi Urban Shelter Improvement Board (DUSIB) had provided. . . . Yet, everything changed on the night of March 9. . . . That's when bulldozers, in the presence of police, demolished temporary shelters, . . . Now, . . . about 1,200 people who used to live in four-night shelters, sit under the sky.

In the final analysis, one must not find fault with any government agency with emotion sans evidence. As noted in Annex 5, there have been several government initiatives (central and state[20] levels) for providing housing for the economically weaker sections of the population.

2.4 Criticality of Housing for Health

Based on the data on water, sanitation, and health indicators, 2022 (Table 1 of the Statistical Annex), a set of correlations are worked out using the cross-country data for the 17 nations in focus (Table 2.6 has the results).

Better sanitation, water access, and water quality help reduce undernourishment. *Responses to water quality and subjective satisfaction about health*

Table 2.6 Correlations from cross-country data

Percentage or proportion of population	Sanitation	Water access	Water quality	Health care*
Undernourished (%)	−0.65	−0.72	−0.66	−0.27
Improved sanitation (proportion)		0.75	0.49	0.13
Water access (Proportion)			0.45	0.17
Water quality (proportion)				**0.82**

* Satisfaction with the availability of quality healthcare (proportion of population)

care are highly positively linked. This reflects the criticality of quality water for ensuring good health. It is a further demonstration of the importance of decent housing and living conditions.

2.5 Visible Equality

It is often said that where there is a will, there is the way. This is so in respect of Singapore government housing. This section/chapter ends with drawing the policy lesson from the Singapore case. (Note: Google search for "countries promoting housing complexes to unite different ethnic groups or income classes or people of different colour" did not bring out any results; instead, the search has only given cases of disparities.)

2.5.1 The Singapore Case

The site www.gov.sg/ (accessed June 26, 2023) has the article "HDB's Ethnic Integration Policy: Why It Still Matters" (published April 13, 2020). HDB stands for the Housing and Development Board of Singapore. The Ethnic Integration Policy or EIP "applies to the sale and purchase of all new and resale HDB flats, as well as the allocation of rental flats by HDB". Here is a quotable quote from the aforementioned article:

It was introduced in 1989 to ensure a balanced mix of ethnic groups in HDB estates, and to prevent the formation of racial enclaves. It seeks to promote racial integration in Singapore by allowing residents of different ethnicities to live together and interact on a regular basis in public housing, where 80% of the population lives.

Undoubtedly, Singapore's HDB promoted visible equality via the EIP.

2.5.2 All Countries Could Emulate

Visible inequality is well known: sprawling bungalows (some with own swimming pools) in one estate for those who wish to showcase their wealth, as against far-off locales with the poor and low-income housing. *Such visible inequality can be written off with two simple rules: all land belongs to the nation at large; and an appropriate EIP applies to all.*

Where colour is the presiding factor as in the United States, the focus of EIP will be on the broad preservation of the ethnic proportions. In nations like India where diversity is far different with different languages and castes, Ethnic Integration Policy will have to take a different form – something like VEP or visible equality policy.

In regard to large cities, the best is to ensure that those below the poverty line have provisions within each housing complex – with eventual dilution of the idea of one *habitat* for the rich and another for the poor. The idea is not to ensure bungalows for one and all; it is to encourage builders of housing estates to make two bedroom apartments on the four sides of a compound wall to accommodate families of security staff, maids, nurses, cleaners, etc.[21]

Notes

1 Lalueza-Fox, Carles (2022), *Inequality: A Genetic History*, The MIT Press.
2 The case is for a humanity-centred globalization with due respect for the environment. See Norman, Donald A. (2023), *Design for a Better World: Meaningful, Sustainable, Humanity Centered*, The MIT Press. A key issue addressed in the book is how to overcome the harmful effects of commerce and manufacturing via a recalibration of what the global populations consider important in life.
3 Schwartz, Alex F. (2021), *Housing Policy in the United States*, Routledge. The quote in the text is based on www.taylorfrancis.com/books/mono/10.4324/9781003097501/housing-policy-united-states-alex-schwartz (Accessed June 27, 2023).
4 The housing–health connection has been duly explored in the Baker, Emma and Bentley, Rebecca (Eds.) (2023), "Housing, Inequality, and Health", *International Journal of Housing Policy*, 23(2), Special Issue. See also Korver-Glenn, Elizabeth, Locklear, Sofia, Howell, Junia and Whitehead, Ellen (2023), "Displaced and Unsafe: The Legacy of Settler-Colonial Racial Capitalism in the U.S. Rental Market", *Journal of Race, Ethnicity, and the City*, 1–22.
5 https://dcist.com/story/23/05/10/dc-region-increase-homelessness/ (Accessed June 23, 2023).
6 The count is imperfect, with outcomes hinging in part on the weather at the time of the count and the number of shelter beds available in any given jurisdiction; it also doesn't account for a variety of populations experiencing housing instability, including those couch-surfing with friends or experiencing a time-limited rental subsidy.

(source as note 5). See also Winegarden, Wayne, et al. (2021),
*No Way Home: The Crisis of Homelessness and How to Fix It with
Intelligence and Humanity*, Encounter Books.

7 Though not directly related to the DC area, it is worth mentioning the New York Times journalist Conor Dougherty's book (*Golden Gates: The Housing Crisis and*

a Reckoning for the American Dream, Penguin Books, 2021). Here is a quote about the book on the amazon.com site:

Spacious and affordable homes used to be the hallmark of American prosperity. Today, however, punishing rents and the increasingly prohibitive cost of ownership have turned housing into the foremost symbol of inequality and an economy gone wrong. Nowhere is this more visible than in the San Francisco Bay Area, where fleets of private buses ferry software engineers past the tarp-and-plywood shanties of the homeless. The adage that California is a glimpse of the nation's future has become a cautionary tale.

(www.amazon.com/Golden-Gates-Housing-Reckoning-American/dp/0525560238 (Accessed June 27, 2023)).

8 Li, Chunling and Fan, Yiming (2020), "Housing Wealth Inequality in Urban China: The Transition from Welfare Allocation to Market Differentiation", *The Journal of Chinese Sociology*, 7, Article number 16.

9 There is, however, some degree of policy intervention.

In 2014, the Interim Measure for Social Assistance was released, and the housing assistance system became a nationwide policy. . . . Local governments give priority to allocate the public rental housing, grant rental subsides for the low-income families in housing difficulties in urban areas and give priority to include them into the project to renovate dilapidated houses and renovate their houses as early as possible in rural areas.

– from Lixiong, Yang (2018), *The Social Assistance Reform in China: Towards a Fair and Inclusive Social Safety Net*, Paper for the Conference on "Addressing Inequalities and Challenges to Social Inclusion through Fiscal, Wage and Social Protection Policies", United Nations, June 25–27.

10 "Where Do the Richest Chinese Live in China?", *Mansion Global*, October 12, 2017.

11 *Caixin Global*, October 2, 2017.

12 Huang, Tianlei (2023), *Why China's Housing Policies Have Failed*, Working Papers 23–25, Peterson Institute for International Economics, June, p. 19.

13 Ibid., p. 41.

14 Data are from the Beijing Statistical Yearbook, 2022.

15 www.jll.co.in/en/trends-and-insights/research/surging-land-acquisitions-in-delhi-ncr (Accessed July 8, 2023).

16 Government of NCT of Delhi, Directorate of Economics & Statistics (2021), *Drinking Water, Sanitation, Hygiene and Housing Condition in Delhi, Based on the State Sample of the National Sample Survey, July 2018 – December 2018*, Government of NCT of Delhi, Directorate of Economics & Statistics, September 2021.

17 Government of NCT of Delhi, Directorate of Economics & Statistics (2020), *Report on Socio-Economic Profile of Residents of Delhi (Part 1: Households Characteristics)*, Government of NCT of Delhi, Directorate of Economics & Statistics, March.

18 The time period covered is November 2018 through November 2019.

19 Government of NCT of Delhi, Directorate of Economics & Statistics (2020), *Report on Socio-Economic Profile of Residents of Delhi (Part 1: Households Characteristics)*, Government of NCT of Delhi, Directorate of Economics & Statistics, p. 12.

20 *The Hindustan Times* of June 22, 2023, reported about the inauguration of a housing complex built by the Telangana State. Considered the largest government-built housing complex in Asia, it comprises 15,660 double bedroom flats in 117 blocks. The flats are for allotment to the deserving below poverty line households.

21 When the principal author suggested along these lines to one of the directors of a construction company in India, his reaction was simple and straight: "cannot be done for two reasons: demand for our villas will drop and we face a price fall". Unless governments take policy action, visible equality in housing will not happen.

3 Health

3.1 Cross-country Trends

Developments of vaccines and medicines happening continuously helped in achieving significant improvements in life expectancy: between 1990 and 2020, from 50 years to 62 in the low-income countries, 59 to 67 in lower-middle, 68 to 75 in upper-middle, and 75 to 80 years in the high-income countries.[1] Also, there has been access to health care on a much better footing today.

However, that is not the same as visibility of equality in the health system: rich and poor alike having access to any hospital and any doctor as per choice and need. Table 3.1 showcases the ground reality in respect of the 17 countries in focus. Japan has the highest score and Bangladesh the lowest.

Table 3.2 brings out the evidence on how the advanced nations such as the United States and Japan minimize the out-of-pocket expense of patients, while in 11 out of the 17 countries, patients take a third to three quarters of the burden.

Based on the data in Table 2 of the Statistical Annex, the following correlations were found: −0.60 between the percentage of out-of-pocket expense and physicians per thousand people and −0.75 between out-of-pocket expense and nurses and midwives per thousand people. The correlations may be interpreted as follows: policy initiatives promoting free health care for increasing numbers would reduce the medical spending from people's pockets and necessitate a growing medical manpower.

In the olden days, people were scared about the incidence of tuberculosis (TB). Today, it has been well controlled. Sad to say, TB is still a health threat in many low- and middle-income countries. Additionally, there is diabetes, which seems not to discriminate between rich and not rich nations. As evidenced from the data in Table 3.3, the control of TB does not mean control of other diseases like diabetes. Thus, while the United States has record low incidence of TB, it is the some of the low-income African nations that have very low diabetes incidence.

Of note too is the fact that good sanitation and good water as well as good ratings on health care services do not add up to reduced incidence of TB and diabetes, as indicated by near zero or extremely low correlations between TB/diabetes and the indicators in Table 1 of the Statistical Annex: access to

DOI: 10.4324/9780429059629-3

Table 3.1 Equal access to quality healthcare, 2022 [Score 0 (completely unequal); score 4 (fully equal)]

Country	Score	Country	Score
Japan	3.9	Ethiopia	1.1
Vietnam	2.5	India	1.0
Russia	2.5	Congo, DR	0.9
Iran	2.3	The Philippines	0.8
The United States	2.1	Mexico	0.8
Indonesia	1.7	Nigeria	0.8
Brazil	1.3	Egypt	0.7
Pakistan	1.2	Bangladesh	0.3
China	1.2		

Source: Social Progress Index. The data in the table is a condensed form of the original data in SPI (see Annex 3 for more details).

Table 3.2 Percentage of out-of-pocket expense in total medical cost, 2022

Country	Percentage	Country	Percentage
The United States	9.9	Mexico	38.8
Japan	12.6	Vietnam	39.6
Brazil	22.4	Congo, DR	39.7
Russia	27.8	The Philippines	45.0
Indonesia	31.8	India	50.6
Ethiopia	33.1	Pakistan	55.4
China	34.8	Egypt	59.3
Iran	37.1	Bangladesh	74.0
		Nigeria	74.7

Source: Social Progress Index.

Table 3.3 Incidence of tuberculosis and diabetes (TB per 100,000 people and diabetes % in 20–79 aged population)

Country	TB	Diabetes	Country	TB	Diabetes
The United States	3	11	Ethiopia	119	5
Egypt	10	21	Vietnam	173	6
Japan	11	7	India	210	10
Iran	12	9	Nigeria	219	4
Mexico	25	17	Bangladesh	221	14
Russia	47	6	Pakistan	264	31
Brazil	48	9	Congo, DR	318	6
China	55	11	Indonesia	354	11
			The Philippines	650	7

improved sanitation, satisfaction with water quality, and satisfaction with the availability of quality healthcare. *The message is clear: there are no shortcuts to ensuring healthy lives for the people of a nation. Excellent health care alone can help.*

3.2 Right to Health

Based on the information at www.ohchr.org/en/health (accessed July 16, 2023), the right to health has the following components: availability, accessibility, acceptability, quality, participation, and accountability. OHCHR'S role in promoting the right to health has many dimensions. These include providing technical assistance and advice to countries and other stakeholders, advocating for the empowerment of rights holders to claim their health-related rights, and promoting the right to health for persons with disabilities.

3.2.1 Special Rapporteur on the Right to Health

"The Special Rapporteur has been mandated to pay attention to groups in vulnerable or marginalized situations, to apply a gender perspective, and to address the needs of children in the realization of the right to health" (taken from the site noted earlier). The key activities of the Special Rapporteur include the following: presenting annual reports to the Human Rights Council and the UN General Assembly on the activities and studies undertaken *and* monitoring the situation of the right to health throughout the world. The Rapporteur[2] communicates to the states and other concerned parties regarding alleged cases of violations of the right to health, etc.

3.2.2 UHC: An Overview

In June 2023, the UN's OHCHR brought out a four-page Overview on Universal Health Coverage and the Right to Health. As part of the Sustainable Development Goals, there is the commitment on universal health coverage (UHC) by 2030 to ensure that "all people have access to essential health services without suffering financial hardship" (*Overview*, p. 1).

> As per the *Overview* document, the following are the key actions necessary to ensure a *human rights-based approach to the provision of Universal Health Coverage (UHC*1. Prioritize populations that are most left behind; 2. Include coverage for essential services; 3. Proactively increase resources available for health services; 4. Remove non-financial barriers to health services; *and* 5. Ensure an inclusive, transparent, and accountable process.

In regard to the first action, the *Overview* makes the following key points: for the poorest of the population, health services and medicines must be provided completely free of charge; countries should rely on domestic resources and general taxation, such as progressive income taxes, to fund UHC.

As for increasing resources for health (the third action), the following are suggested: "increasing allocations to health from national budgets, improving tax collection, combating tax avoidance, introducing anti-corruption efforts to free up additional resources for health budgets, and seeking debt relief or international assistance" (*Overview* page 3).

3.3 Case Studies of Four Countries

This section showcases the health care systems of India and China, with the largest population sizes; and Japan and the United States in the top health system rank among the 17 countries in focus.[3]

3.3.1 India

From the Executive Summary of a recent WHO publication,[4] the key points on the country's health care system are noted next.

*India achieved infant mortality rate (IMR) reduction from 88 per 1,000 live births in 1990 to about 32 in 2020. Similarly, the maternal mortality ratio (MMR) declined from 556 in 1990 to 113 per 100,000 live births during 2016–2018, *but the progress has been uneven with economically weaker states continuing to report higher rates.*

*India's health care system helped eradicating some communicable diseases such as polio. However, TB and other challenges continue. Noncommunicable diseases and injuries together account for over half the disease burden.

**Out-of-pocket spending accounts for nearly two-thirds of total health spending, leading to over 55 million people going into poverty every year.*

*Access to medicines and medical equipment in government health facilities remains poor. It is not just supply of medicines; the issue of quality is critical as well.[5]

*Two of the earlier initiatives have been the National Rural Health Mission/ National Health Mission (NRHM/NHM), primarily geared to addressing maternal and neonatal conditions, and various infectious disease control programmes. NHM's focus on expanding institutional deliveries helped in raising the share of deliveries in health facilities, from 43% in 2004 to 83% in 2018, with a sizeable rise in the share of deliveries in government health facilities (21% to 53%).

3.3.1.1 Health and Wellness Centres

In 2018 February, Government of India announced Ayushman Bharat (AB) Programme. What follows is based on the comprehensive information at the site https://ab-hwc.nhp.gov.in/. AB has two components which are complementary to each other. Under its first component, 150,000 Health and Wellness Centres (HWCs) will deliver comprehensive primary health care, that is universal and free to users. The focus is on wellness and the delivery of an expanded range of services[6] closer to the community. The second component is the Pradhan Mantri Jan Arogya Yojana (PM-JAY) which provides health insurance cover of Rs 5 lakhs per year to over 10 crore poor and vulnerable families for seeking secondary and tertiary care.

3.3.1.2 An Optimistic Note

As of July 19, 2023, there are 1,60,365 functional HWCs. Their efficiency and the resulting health progress need to be independently monitored, and corrective actions should be taken as needed. If all goes well, India could be a global inspiration to ensure good health to the poor and vulnerable.

3.3.2 China

China's basic health insurance system covers over 95% of the population.[7] In 2018, the National Healthcare Security Administration was established, managing all basic health insurance schemes in China. Its establishment is a milestone in China's health sector reform and represents opportunities to further improve the efficiency of the health system on cost containment, quality of services, and better value for money.

3.3.2.1 Encouraging Results

In the decade 2009–2018, government health expenditure more than tripled; and households' out-of-pocket expenditure in total health expenditure dropped from 37.5% to 28.6%.

China's basic medical insurance includes two systems: employee medical insurance and resident medical insurance. The first covers urban employed population, while the second caters to urban non-employed and rural populations. There is, however, one limitation: public health insurance generally only covers about half of medical costs, with the proportion lower for serious or chronic illnesses. Under the "Healthy China 2020" initiative,[8] China has undertaken an effort to cut healthcare costs.

China maintains parallelly modern or Western medicine, as well as its traditional Chinese medicine (TCM). Some Chinese consider TCM backward and ineffective; others consider it inexpensive, effective, and culturally appropriate. China has also become a major market for health-related multinational companies.

According to a 2022 January research paper,[9] satisfaction with health care increased from 57.8% to 77.3%, and perceived fairness from about 50% to 72% between 2006 and 2019.

3.3.2.2 Not Everything is OK

There are concerns that need to be addressed, as succinctly pointed out in a recent publication.[10] The gap between demand and supply of healthcare is expanding (due to increasing aged population and rising expectations). The problems include an insufficient medical insurance fund, nonuniform insurance reimbursement policies, a poor integrity system, and a lack of supervision in the management of the medical insurance fund.

The paper under reference points to some practical solutions worth considering: a national medical insurance supervision platform to be continuously strengthened; blacklisting illegal medical institutions and individuals engaged in malicious medical practices; and policies to narrow the differences in regional medical insurance policies and reimbursement levels of residents in the different regions. Of utmost priority is addressing the regional disparities in infrastructure and facilities.

> High-quality medical resources are mainly concentrated in large and medium-sized cities. . . . Most of the top 100 hospitals in northern China are concentrated in Beijing. The top hospitals in the western region are concentrated in Xi'an, Chengdu, and Chongqing. Although the economy in South China is relatively developed, medical resources are mainly concentrated in Changsha, Wuhan, and Guangzhou. The number of hospitals in Hainan Province is relatively small.[11]

3.3.3 Japan

Globally highly rated, the Japanese health care system has the following important features.[12] Taxes and individual contributions fund health insurance system in Japan, providing universal health coverage for citizens and expatriates. Benefits and fee schedule are set by the Japanese government and are renewed two years once.

> Insured residents pay 30% (children, elderly, and low-income citizens have lower coinsurance rates) of their medical and pharmaceutical costs and the insurer covers the rest, up to monthly and annual maximum limits. . . . The universal healthcare reimbursement system evaluates the services provided by each facility so that services are maintained at a high level across the country.[13]

The efficacy of the Japanese health care system is reflected in the fact that the country has a very high life expectancy of 85 years in 2023.

3.3.3.1 Japan Council for Quality Health Care (JQ)[14]

Added to the government's role, the work of the Japan Council for Quality Health Care (JQ) has also helped in ensuring high standards.

Established in 1995 as an independent, non-profit organization, JQ's aim is "to contribute to the improvement of the health and welfare of the public and, as a neutral and scientific third-party organization, carries out projects to improve the quality of healthcare and ensure reliable healthcare". The values of JQ include "creating relationships of trust with patients, families, healthcare providers and all related parties, . . . ; and preserving complete fairness and impartiality". A key activity undertaken by JQ is hospital accreditation. JQ's website provides links to Hospital Accreditation Standards covering diverse hospitals.

3.3.3.2 The Challenges Ahead

https://healthsystemsfacts.org/ (accessed July 20, 2023) provides several interesting metrics on the Japanese health care system. Population size was 124 million in mid-2022, with 30% aged 65 years and over. Two of the core demographic features in the future happen to be slowly declining population and rising aged proportions. The *Japan Health System Review*,[15] a WHO publication, succinctly points to the upcoming healthcare challenges. Universal health insurance, insured's freedom to choose health care facilities, and ensuring good quality care at an affordable price – all these necessitated tight controls of health-care costs.

> [A] laissez-faire approach to service delivery, with inadequate governance of provider organisations, created a mismatch between need and supply of health-care resources and impeded accountability for care quality. Japan's economic slowdown, high life expectancy, and growing use of expensive technologies have led to an ever-increasing rate of health-care expenditure.[16]

3.3.3.3 Japan Vision: Healthcare 2035

In 2015, Japan's Ministry of Health, Labour and Welfare constituted an Expert Advisory Panel to focus on *Japan Vision: Healthcare 2035* and suggest ways to meet the challenges facing the country's healthcare system. By June 2015, the Panel brought out its report. The following are some of the key points noted in the executive summary.[17] *A paradigm shift is envisaged from: quantity to quality, inputs to value, government regulation to autonomy, cure to care, and fragmentation to integration.*

Among the goals for 2035, following are noteworthy: achieve a "tobacco-free" society by 2035; support the widespread use of a portable information infrastructure that includes long-term care information; provide the public with one-stop, holistic health and lifestyle services that integrate multiple fields of care to support autonomy and agency in health: and build communities from a social determinants of health (SDH) perspective. As part of the overall hard and soft infrastructure targets, two are especially noteworthy: establishing a financial support mechanism to complement public insurance and transferring authority to prefectures so that regional disparities can be addressed.

3.3.3.4 A Postscript

The world will be watching the Japanese experience on building an effective healthcare system in the coming decades – in the background of falling population size, rising ageing, constraints on economic growth, and limitations on fiscal resources. Many countries that will take the same route in the decades to come will benefit from the Japanese experience.

3.3.4 The United States

Table 5 in the Statistical Annex provides cross-country data on the percentage of GDP spent on health expenditure – averages for 2000–2009, 2010–2019, and 2020. Among the 17 countries in focus, the United States has the highest percentages – 14.4%, 16.4%, and 18.8% respectively in the three periods. Despite this accomplishment, health problems continue to be a major concern.

3.3.4.1 From the Commonwealth Fund

The Commonwealth Fund[18] Commission on a National Public Health System in its report,[19] brought out in June 2022, briefly showcases the health challenges such as the following. More than a million Americans died from COVID-19. In 2021, over 100,000 died from drug overdoses. The HIV epidemic continues to claim thousands of lives. Maternal mortality is rising, with black women three times more likely to die from a pregnancy-related cause than white women. Far too many people suffer from preventable cancers. *Trends such as these are behind the low life expectancy rank of the United States – 64 as shown in Table 6 of the Statistical Annex, with some of the "developing" countries occupying higher spots.*

The Commonwealth Fund Report is laudable for its brevity and clarity, whole report occupying 30 pages and Executive Summary taking just one page.[20] The expert committee that worked on the report has a chairperson and eight members – all highly qualified and distinguished in the health field. *They set a great example for all committees and experts to follow – brevity not verbosity.*

The following are extracts from the executive summary.

The key issues and needs are as follows: An overall leading and coordinating office is not in place to guide and monitor the work of the dozens of federal health agencies and nearly 3,000 state, local, tribal, and territorial health departments. The chronic underfunding of public health has left behind a weak infrastructure (data systems, labs, and workforce). Funding is not linked to expected results. Racism, discrimination, misinformation, and the likes are behind lack of trust in the system.

The Commission's main recommendation is that "The United States should build a national public health system to promote and protect the health of every person, regardless of who they are and where they live".

To reach that goal and maintain it, the Commission recommended several initiatives such as the following: *The US Congress* should "Establish a position, such as an undersecretary for public health at the U.S. Department of Health and Human Services (HHS), to oversee and coordinate the development of the national public health system".

Positions and structures without funding are of little benefit, and, hence, the Congress must "Provide adequate and reliable public health infrastructure funding, paired with expectations that states, localities, tribes, and territories meet standards for protecting their communities".

Several suggestions were also made regarding the administrative operationalization of the broad objectives. *It is now a matter of wait and watch for the federal and state governments to take the suggested actions.*

3.4 SDG: Health Goals, Targets, and Progress

The Sustainable Development Goal number 3 is Good Health and Well-Being: *ensure healthy lives and promote well-being for all at all ages.* The following are the specific targets *to be achieved by 2030:*

• Reducing the global maternal mortality ratio to less than 70 per 100,000 live births; ending preventable deaths of newborns and children under five years of age, with all countries aiming to reduce neonatal mortality to at least as low as 12 per 1,000 live births and under-5 mortality to at least as low as 25 per 1,000 live births.

- Ending the epidemics of AIDS, tuberculosis, malaria and neglected tropical diseases and combat hepatitis, water-borne diseases, and other communicable diseases.
- Ensuring universal access to sexual and reproductive health-care services, including for family planning, information, and education, and the integration of reproductive health into national strategies and programmes.
- Achieving universal health coverage, including financial risk protection; access to quality essential health-care services; and access to safe, effective, quality and affordable essential medicines and vaccines for all.
- Substantially reduce the number of deaths and illnesses from hazardous chemicals and air, water, and soil pollution and contamination.

3.4.1 The Sustainable Development Goals Report 2022[21]

Issued in July 2022, the Sustainable Development Goals Report 2022 provides a global overview of progress in the aftermath of the COVID pandemic.

> The Report details the reversal of years of progress in eradicating poverty and hunger, improving health and education, providing basic services, and much more. It also points out areas that need urgent action in order to rescue the SDGs and deliver meaningful progress for people and the planet by 2030.

The four pages (30–33) dealing with progress on good health and well-being contain the following points: COVID-19 directly and indirectly led to the *deaths of nearly 15 million people* in the first two years of the pandemic. The pandemic caused a rise in anxiety and depression, particularly among young people. Despite progress in maternal and child health, glaring regional disparities persist and need to be addressed. Progress towards universal health coverage was affected by COVID-19 and related developments. Progress against HIV, tuberculosis and malaria was also adversely affected. More and more children are missing out on essential vaccines. Health and care workers were adversely affected.

3.5 Moving Forward

An enterprise must not look at auditor reports as a mere formality to follow the set rules promulgated by a government. An honest report by a qualified and experienced auditor helps to correct the inadequate business practices and close the gaps in reporting if any. The same analogy should apply to the work of the United Nations agencies.

The whole world will be a great place to live well and securely when the SDGs are fully achieved by 2030. Even if success is on the anvil, new health challenges will keep coming; and of course, there will be plenty of room for more meetings and reports by UN organs. While waiting for all these year after year and decade after decade, a worthy initiative by the UN may be considered as discussed next.

3.5.1 Global Health Fund

Globally, the Universal Health Care becomes fully operational if the people of the whole world get identical health care. For this, all the nations must come together and work to create a Global Health Fund (GHF), with the mandate for each and every individual to have a *Global Health Card (GHC)*. Doctors, specialists, nurses, care givers, etc., get the same pay and benefits *in real terms* across the world. The UN and WHO should work out the full operational details of GHF and GHC.

> *Health is real wealth. If the august world bodies can help in bringing people together via guaranteed healthcare of the same quality across the world, it is a monumental accomplishment. Generations of global citizens will celebrate full visibility of equality on the health care front, recalling the great efforts of their predecessors.*

Notes

1 Data source: World Development Indicators.
2 Ms. Tlaleng Mofokeng, from South Africa, is the present Special Rapporteur (noted in July 2023).
3 See Table 4 of the Statistical Annex.
4 Selvaraj, S., Karan, K.A., Srivastava, Swati, Bhan, Nandita and Mukhopadhyay, Indranil (2022), *India Health System Review*, World Health Organization, Regional Office for South-East Asia. Pages 1 through 6 contain the Executive Summary.
5 To understand the issue of quality and the key role of regulation, see Thakur, Dinesh Singh, and Prashant, Reddy (2022), *The Truth Pill: The Myth of Drug Regulation in India*, Simon & Schuster.
6 The services go beyond maternal and child health care services to include care for non-communicable diseases; palliative and rehabilitative care; oral, eye and ENT care; mental health; and first-level care for emergencies and trauma, including free essential drugs and diagnostic services.
7 www.who.int/china/health-topics/health-financing (Accessed July 19, 2023).
8 https://en.wikipedia.org/wiki/Healthcare_in_China (Accessed July 19, 2023).
9 Zhu, Yishan, et al. (2022), "How Do Chinese People Perceive Their Healthcare System? Trends and Determinants of Public Satisfaction and Perceived Fairness, 2006–2019", *BMC Health Services Research*, 22.
10 Chen, Cui and Liu, Mao (2023), "Achievements and Challenges of the Healthcare System in China", *Cureus*, 15(5), e39030, May 15.

11 Ibid.

12 Kondo, Tatsuya and MEJ Four-Dimensional Health Innovation Group (2022), "Report on the Nature, Characteristics, and Outcomes of the Japanese Healthcare System", *Global Health & Medicine*, 4(1), 37–44, February 28.

13 Ibid.

14 This sub-section is based on the information at https://jcqhc.or.jp/en/ (Accessed July 20, 2023).

15 Sakamoto, Haruka, et al. (2018), *Japan Health System Review*, vol. 8, no. 1, World Health Organization, Regional Office for South-East Asia (The core messages are from the Executive Summary).

16 Ibid.

17 www.mhlw.go.jp/healthcare2035.

18 Established in 1918 by a highly motivated philanthropical lady, the Commonwealth Fund's key objective is ensuring the best of health for one and all in the world at large.

19 The Commonwealth Fund Commission on a National Public Health System (2022), *Meeting America's Public Health Challenge: Recommendations for Building a National Public Health System That Addresses Ongoing and Future Health Crises, Advances Equity, and Earns Trust*, The Commonwealth Fund, June.

20 Chair: Margaret A. Hamburg, M.D. [Former Commissioner of Food and Drugs; former Assistant Secretary for Planning and Evaluation; former Commissioner, New York City Department of Health and Mental Hygiene]; members: Mandy Cohen, M.D., M.P.H [Former Secretary of the North Carolina Department of Health and Human Services]; Karen DeSalvo, M.D., M.P.H., M.Sc. [Former U.S. Assistant Secretary for Health (Acting) and former National Coordinator for Health Information Technology; former New Orleans Commissioner of Health]; Julie Gerberding, M.D., M.P.H. [Former Director, U.S. Centers for Disease Control and Prevention]; Joneigh Khaldun, M.D., M.P.H. [Appointee, Presidential COVID-19 Health Equity Task Force; former Chief Medical Executive, State of Michigan; former Detroit Health Commissioner; former Chief Medical Officer, Baltimore City Health Department]; David Lakey, M.D. [Vice Chancellor for Health Affairs and Chief Medical Officer, the University of Texas System; former Texas Commissioner of Health; past President of the Association of State and Territorial Health Officials]; Ellen MacKenzie, Ph.D., Sc.M. [Dean, Johns Hopkins Bloomberg School of Public Health]; Herminia Palacio, M.D., M.P.H. [President & CEO, Guttmacher Institute; former New York City Deputy Mayor for Health and Human Services; former Executive Director and Local Health Authority, Harris County (TX) Public Health and Environmental Services]; and Nirav R. Shah, M.D., M.P.H. [Senior Scholar, Clinical Excellence Research Center, Stanford University; Chief Medical Officer, American Health Associates; former Commissioner of Health, State of New York].

21 United Nations publication issued by the Department of Economic and Social Affairs (DESA), 2022.

4 Education

4.1 Introduction

The focus of this chapter is on the first 12 years of education, popularly known as school education, which is the foundation for higher education, for equalizing opportunity, and progress over one's lifespan. School education focuses on and improves the communication and analytical capabilities and injects scientific and innovative zeal.

In any country, if every child has free access to the 12 years of excellent primary, secondary, and higher secondary education, that would be equalizing opportunity in the true sense.

4.2 Cross-country Trends

4.2.1 Equality of Access

At the outset, one can see the ground reality on educational access from the data in Table 4.1, which covers the 17 countries in focus. Equality of access perception score is the highest for Japan and close to 0 in the case of Pakistan. As a free country with 1.4 billion people, India should have focussed on equalizing access, but the reality is far different.

Equal access would, over time, minimize the population with no education. This can be seen from Table 4.2 which has the cross-country data on the percentage of population with no education arranged in ascending order. For instance, Japan is in the top position in both Tables 4.1 and 4.2. However, the cross-country inter-correlation was only −0.6 between the access perception scores and population percentages with no education. This not-so-high correlation could be in part due to the subjective nature of the perception score.

4.2.2 Women with Advanced Education

Of great importance and significance is the education of women. Families and nations would benefit greatly if every woman were highly educated. It would also greatly enhance gender equality.

DOI: 10.4324/9780429059629-4

Table 4.1 Extent of equality in access to quality education, 2022 (Scale 0 to 4 representing "fully unequal" to "totally equal")

Country	Score	Country	Score
Japan	**3.9**	Mexico	1.0
Vietnam	2.6	Indonesia	1.0
Russia	2.4	The Philippines	0.9
Iran	2.4	India	0.9
The United States	2.4	Nigeria	0.7
Ethiopia	1.6	Brazil	0.7
China	1.6	Bangladesh	0.7
Congo, DR	1.3	Egypt	0.4
		Pakistan	0.2

Source: Social Progress Index (see Annex 3 for more details).

Table 4.2 Percentage of population with no schooling, 2022

Country	%	Country	%
Japan	0.1	Mexico	7.5
Russia	0.2	Brazil	8.8
The United States	0.6	Congo, DR	15.4
The Philippines	3.2	Egypt	19.2
Vietnam	4.3	Iran	24.1
Ethiopia	5.3	India	29.8
China	6.9	Bangladesh	30.4
Indonesia	7.2	Nigeria	32.6
		Pakistan	39.3

Source: Social Progress Index.

Table 4.3 has the 17 countries arranged in the descending order of the percentage of women with advanced education. The United States, Russia, and Japan are in the top league. There is a distinct drop after Japan, with the Philippines and Egypt recording a little less than half the women having advanced education.

4.2.3 On the PISA Scale

PISA (Programme for International Student Assessment) began in the year 2000. It aims to evaluate education systems worldwide by testing the skills and knowledge of 15-year-old students in participating countries/economies. Table 4.4 has data for 2018 on the percentage of students with lowest proficiency in mathematics and science. Kudos to the students of China, with none in math and science with the lowest proficiency. Their performance is well above that of the US students.

Table 4.3 The percentage of women with advanced education, 2022

Country	%	Country	%
The United States	83.2	Vietnam	34.2
Russia	79.2	Nigeria	25.3
Japan	76.9	Brazil	23.6
The Philippines	46.8	Mexico	23.4
Egypt	46.3	India	19.9
Iran	37.2	Congo, DR	17.8
Indonesia	34.5	Pakistan	10.7
China	34.4	Bangladesh	10.7
		Ethiopia	3.8

Source: Social Progress Index (see Annex 1.3 for more details).

Table 4.4 Students at lowest proficiency on PISA (% of 15-year-olds, 2018)

Country	Mathematics	Science
China	0	0
Japan	3	0
Vietnam	3	0
Russia	7	0
The United States	10	1
Mexico	26	1
Brazil	41	4
Indonesia	41	2
The Philippines	54	7

Note: *Countries with no data:*
Bangladesh; Congo, DR; Egypt; Ethiopia; India; Iran; Nigeria; and Pakistan

It is of note that India is among the nations with no data. Here is a pertinent comment from *The Economist* on the education system of the country:

> As the rich world and China grow older, India's huge youth bulge – some 500m of its people are under 20 – should be an additional propellant. Yet as we report, . . . education for most Indians is still a bust. Unskilled, jobless youngsters risk bringing India's economic development to a premature stop.[1]

4.2.4 Secondary School Pupil–Teacher Ratio

Table 4.5 has the secondary school pupil–teacher ratios for 11 countries. China stands out for two reasons: low ratio to begin with and decline over time. As noted earlier in the comment from *The Economist*, India's relatively high ratio does not augur well for its demographic dividend.

Table 4.5 Secondary school pupil–teacher ratio, 2000, 2010, and 2018

Country	2000	2010	2018	Country	2000	2010	2018
Bangladesh	38	28	35	Indonesia	15	12	15
Brazil		17		India	34	25	28
China	*17*	*15*	*13*	Mexico	17	18	
Congo, DR		16		Nigeria	31	23	
Egypt	17		15	Pakistan			20
Ethiopia		43					

Note: No data for Iran, Japan, the Philippines, Russia, the United States, and Vietnam

Table 4.6 Percentage of first graders reaching grade 5

Country	Males		Females	
	2015	2020	2015	2020
China	..	100	..	100
Congo, DR	*45*	..	*68*	..
Egypt	97	99	98	100
Ethiopia	*43*	*40*	*45*	*41*
India	89	86	91	87
Indonesia	98	..	100	..
Iran	97	..	100	..
Pakistan	79	61	75	71
The Philippines	93	97	96	99
Russia	..	..	..	..
The United States	..	96	..	91
Vietnam	94	..	*98*	..

Note: No data for Bangladesh, Brazil, Japan, Nigeria, and Russia

4.2.5 Reaching Grade 5

Table 4.6 shows the efficacy of the primary school education system in terms of the percentage of first graders reaching grade 5.

China, in 2020, has the full 100% score for male students as well as female students. Most of the other countries have a 90 or close percentage of first graders reaching grade 5. Congo, DR and Ethiopia have the lowest scores.

4.3 Education: China and Japan

Tables 4.1 and 4.2 draw attention to Japan in the top position. China achieved excellence on PISA and the top score regarding first graders reaching fifth grade. The two country cases in brief are given in the remainder of this section – to help understand the systems behind successes.

4.3.1 China

The following account is based on the most authentic source: the website of China's Ministry of Education (http://en.moe.gov.cn/ accessed July 29, 2023). There are three links that are the sources used here: laws and policies, reports, and statistics.

4.3.1.1 Promoting Private Education

China and private education, on the face of it, look like an unreal combination. An amendment to the regulation on the law promoting private education has come into force on September 1, 2021. The following are some of the key points of the new regulation.

Social organizations and individuals other than State institutions can run private schools of various levels and types. *Private schools should uphold the leadership of the Communist Party.* Running the schools through donations and foundations is encouraged. "Foreign-invested enterprises and social organizations actually controlled by the foreign party may not control or take part in the running of private schools for compulsory education". *The supervisory body of private schools should include representatives of grassroots organizations of the Party.* Fees charged by private schools should be regulated. Provincial-level governments can set up support and incentive measures for the growth of private education.

What the leadership behind the new provisions may not appreciate is how private schools can slowly change the educational atmosphere and in due course create awful visible inequalities.

4.3.1.2 Achievements in Compulsory Education, 2012–2021[2]

The Nine-Year Compulsory Education Act came into force on July 1, 1986. Progress in the decade 2012–21 is briefly reviewed in the rest of this sub-section.

China's compulsory education system comprises 207,000 schools, 158 million students, and 10.6 million teachers. Since 2012, a series of reform measures have been taken to improve equity and quality in compulsory education. For instance, allocations to support compulsory education from the central budget doubled between 2012 and 2021, accounting for more than half of total spending on education.

Eligible students enjoy free tuition, free textbooks, and living allowances. Necessary financial assistance is guaranteed to students from disadvantaged backgrounds. Also, 37 million rural students benefited from the Nutrition Improvement Action Plan.

School infrastructure improvement has received priority during the ten-year period. Floor area per student increased from 3.7 to 5 square meters. The proportion of teachers holding bachelor's degrees or above increased from 47.6% to 77.7%.

Measures taken for improving educational equity include the following: private and public schools launching admission procedures simultaneously, allowing migrant students to study and take exams at the place of their parents' work, and appropriate initiatives to alleviate the academic burden on students.

A Guide to Moral Education for Primary and Secondary Schools was published to facilitate moral education. Vocational learning was rolled out in all schools. According to the National Oversight Report on the Quality of Compulsory Education, about 80% of students had above-average academic performance.

China's educational accomplishments at the national level included the following: pre-school education, though not compulsory, attracted close to 90% enrolment, with almost all in "affordable" kindergartens. In 2022, the completion rate of nine-year compulsory education was 95.5%.

4.3.1.3 Senior Secondary Education

This sub-section draws from "A review of achievements in senior secondary education (2012–2021)", posted on October 22, 2022, on the MoE website.

The gross enrolment rate of senior secondary education across China was 91.4% in 2021, an increase of 6.4 percentage points over 2012. Overall investment in senior secondary education increased by over 100% in 2021 compared to 2012. As per the Central Government decision, public spending per student is to be equal to or more than 1,000 yuan ($150 approximately). Some 20% of all registered senior high school students benefitted from a national student aid system.

In 2021, 100% of regular senior high schools across the country had access to the internet. In addition, 76% of all classrooms have been equipped with multimedia tools.

Moral education has been integrated into all aspects of senior secondary education. Schools have been encouraged to diversify their elective courses and develop their unique strengths in different subjects such as science and technology, the humanities, foreign languages, PE, and arts.

4.3.1.4 Vocational Education

As per the review of achievements in vocational education (2012–2021), posted on October 22, 2022, on the MoE website, vocational education institutions offer some 120,000 programmes. Graduates of vocational schools account for over 70% of new frontline workers in advanced manufacturing, emerging industries, and the IT-powered service sector.

Over 4,500 vocational schools give support to 110,000 primary and secondary schools in offering courses on labour practices and professional skills.

The Law on Vocational Education helped to clarify the objectives of vocational education at different levels. Secondary vocational schools focus on training candidates for higher vocational education. Polytechnics are required to produce graduates capable of serving regional development and industrial upgrading.

Vocational education at the undergraduate level has been developed, aiming to provide degree programmes for vocational students. A total of 1,891 higher education institutions offer degree programmes in the form of continuing education, with registered students accounting for 46.8% of the total number of undergraduates. *In addition, 30 open universities for senior citizens have been established.*

China has established partnerships with over 70 countries and international organizations in expanding bilateral cooperation in vocational education. Over 400 vocational colleges have received a total of 17,000 international students.

4.3.2 Japan

The school system in Japan comprises nursery (for children aged 3 to 6), elementary school (6 to 12), lower secondary (12 to 15), and upper secondary (15 to 18). Elementary school and junior high school/lower secondary school are mandatory in Japan. Almost all those completing lower secondary move on to upper secondary.

"Compared to other OECD countries, Japan's education system is one of the top performers among both youth and the adult population", notes the OECD Directorate for Education and Skills, in its short paper "Education Policy in Japan: Building Bridges Towards 2030".[3]

With a curriculum revised every ten years or so, Japan has established a regular cycle to continuously update it, building on evidence from teaching practices. In the new curricular reform, however, Japan has recognized the need to update teaching and learning to foster competencies for the 21st century. In addition to knowledge, this includes developing cross-curricular skills, such as problem-solving and creativity, and good learning habits. To do so, the new curriculum (implemented from 2020–2022) focuses on using active learning strategies to develop the competencies of students around three pillars: 1. motivation to learn and apply learning to life; 2. acquisition of knowledge and technical skills; and 3. skills to think, make judgements, and express oneself.[4]

4.3.2.1 Disaster Risk Education

Japan has been a country prone to natural disasters. They include earthquakes, tsunamis, torrential rains, and typhoons. Of utmost concern for the safety of its residents, Japan not only took timely steps as needed but also integrated disaster risk education with formal education as noted next briefly.[5]

At primary, lower secondary, and upper secondary schools, the following topics were covered as part of the teaching subjects: the mechanics of running water; earth changes driven by volcanic eruptions, earthquakes, and floods; injury prevention and first aid in times of disaster; first aid training in times of disaster; relationship with nature and science; mechanism of volcanic eruptions and earthquakes; and cooking and living in times of disaster.

Drills for evacuation in case of disaster are part of the physical activities. In addition, drills for evacuation in case of disaster and volunteer activities in times of disaster are also integral to the recreational activities.

4.3.2.2 From the UNICEF–UNESCO Case Study

In October 2021, UNICEF and UNESCO together brought out a very informative and useful Japan Case Study.[6] The study, after detailed analysis, concludes: "Considering the severe impact of the COVID-19 pandemic on the region, Japan's ability to respond has been aided by its high levels of investment in education (in gross terms), as well as the maturity of its system". However, one of the key observations was about the fact that the "pandemic highlighted the low level of readiness to shift learning online". Hence, there is the need for

> much more ramped-up efforts to increase children's access to internet and digital devices at home, improve parent and family ability to support children with at-home learning, increase the number of computers at schools to realize the . . . goal of one computer to one child, and provide additional training to teachers to improve their confidence in using ICT as a tool for their own classes.

4.4 First 12 Years of Education: Key to Equal Opportunity

Wherever private schools dominate, it is natural to expect a reduction in the extent of equality of opportunity. Table 4.7 has the relevant data across the countries in focus. India, Indonesia, and Pakistan stand out with more than a third of enrolment in private schools.

Table 4.7 Percentage of students enrolled in private secondary schools, 2018–2020

Country	2018	2019	2020
Brazil	13.9	14.0	13.8
China	12.8	13.7	14.4
Egypt	7.8	8.4	
Indonesia	**42.1**		
India	**51.1**	**51.9**	**51.4**
Iran			11.1
Japan	20.7	21.1	
Mexico	13.3	12.7	12.9
Nigeria	22.8		
Pakistan	**32.5**	**33.6**	
The Philippines	24.7	24.3	23.9
Russia	1.3	1.5	
The United States	8.9	8.9	8.5

Note: Data are not available in respect of Bangladesh; Congo, DR; Ethiopia; and Vietnam

The case of India is really distressing, with a little over half the students in private schools. An Indian publication *Telegraph Online* published "In private: Editorial on recent growth of private schools" on November 7, 2022. Here is the notable concluding statement:

> Intense competition entangled with economic commitments make students and their parents easy prey to profiteering in the name of lessons, whether inside the school or outside it. The bustling world of private and government schools guarantees neither education nor universal access. Quality and equity are yet to be achieved.

A recent UNESCO report[7] in its foreword has a clear message for all the concerned decision-makers:

> This Report's core recommendation for all education actors to widen their understanding of inclusive education to include all learners, no matter their identity, background or ability comes at an opportune time as the world seeks to rebuild back more inclusive education systems.

The report, quite rightly, argues that education systems should always ensure that learners' interests are placed at the centre. The report further affirms that digital technologies are to support and not replace education based on human interaction.

The ground reality is fully reflected in the following quote from the report: In all but high-income countries in Europe and Northern America, only 18 of the poorest youth complete secondary school for every 100 of the richest youth. Also, students with disabilities do not have special educational facilities in many of the developing nations.[8]

> If governments are keen to promote equality of opportunity, it is crucial that all students are in government schools with standard infrastructure facilities, equally qualified teachers, nationally applicable teacher salaries, and incentives for superior performance.

4.5 Towards A Global Education System

Globalization has been helping to improve foreign direct investment flows leading to production decentralization and promoting international trade, with beneficial effects on transport development, foreign travel, and study abroad. It is time that attempts are made to bring some degree of standardization in educational systems and testing across countries.

4.5.1 *Exams and Tests Galore*

https://en.wikipedia.org/wiki/List_of_secondary_education_systems_by_country (accessed August 3, 2023) provides a whole host of educational institutions and exam types across several countries in the world. That happens to be true even within a country.

In India, for instance, there are tenth and twelfth grade examinations conducted by the various State Boards, the Central Board of Secondary Education (CBSE), the Indian Certificate of Secondary Education (ICSE) Board, the Council for the Indian School Certificate Examination (CISCE), the National Institute of Open Schooling (NIOS), Cambridge International Examinations (CIE), and the IB programme. India's CBSE exams are taken by schools in India as well as 21 countries abroad. Worldwide numerous countries have schools hosting GCE and IB exams, along with their national examination agencies and boards.

4.5.2 *Towards Global Grade Twelve (GGT)*

With a little over 8 billion people living in the world as of August 2023, unifying initiatives help to bring the world together, while dividing efforts succeed in destroying unity.

Education is an important vehicle that can promote or destroy global unity. Languages, cultures, religious orientations, etc., differ across countries; *but science and technology do not differ*. While preserving national and local languages and having examinations relating to them at national/regional/local levels, *every course in science and technology can be based on globally uniform syllabi and texts, with a global exam for them conducted in a decentralized manner.* Since the syllabi are the same, it is just a matter of setting exam papers and practical tests in a broadly comparable fashion facilitating the award of identical pass certificates across the world. *Education ministers across the world should select a team from among them to work out the GGT system details.*

4.5.3 Channelling Education Aid to GGT

The Centre for Global Development[9] has on its website, access to an interesting/enlightening blog post[10] from which one can learn about the reality of educational aid. For instance, US education aid goes mostly to early grade reading and school feeding programmes. In contrast, aid from Germany, France, and Japan goes to post-secondary education, helping students coming to those countries. *In many cases, aid goes to companies and institutions in the donor nations.*

As and when the world goes for GGT, all aid could go into two clear channels: a small portion for GGT implementation and a major part for bringing together the students of different nationalities to countries of their choice to pursue higher education.

4.6 In Tune with SDG

Hoping for the promotion of equality of opportunity is very much in line with the spirit of the Sustainable Development Goal 4 on education: "Ensure inclusive and equitable quality education and promote lifelong learning opportunities for all".

> As long as private schools dominate the educational scene and as long as dozens of national and international tests prevail, inclusiveness shall remain a topic for discourse, continuous research, expert meets, and reports and more reports with no visible equality.

The Global Grade Twelve idea is in tune with the SDG target 4.7:

> By 2030, ensure that all learners acquire the knowledge and skills needed to promote sustainable development, including, among others, through education for sustainable development and sustainable lifestyles, human rights, gender equality, promotion of a culture of peace and non-violence, global citizenship, and appreciation of cultural diversity and of culture's contribution to sustainable development.

It is time that UNESCO takes the lead in universal promotion of government schools as well as a GGT Test, the one test for all.

Notes

1 *The Economist*, July 1, 2023 (Can India educate its vast workforce? Poor schools put the economic boom at risk).

2 As per the report dated October 22, 2023, http://en.moe.gov.cn/ (Accessed July 29, 2023).

3 www.oecd.org/education/Japan-BB2030-Highlights.pdf (Accessed August 2, 2023). See also Yamanaka, Shinichi and Suzuki, Kan Hiroshi (2020), "Japanese Education Reform Towards Twenty-First Century Education", in Reimers, Fernando M. (Ed.) *Audacious Education Purposes*, Springer, pp. 81–103.

4 The Ministry of Education, Culture, Sports, Science and Technology (MEXT) is the Japanese government agency responsible for all decisions and regulations governing education in the country. The website, however, has no updated information. www.mext.go.jp/en/about/mext/index.htm (Accessed August 2, 2023).

5 From Gavari-Starkie, Elisa, Casado-Claro, María-Francisca and Navarro-González, Inmaculada (2021), "The Japanese Educational System as an International Model for Urban Resilience", *International Journal of Environmental Research and Public Health*, 18(11), 5794, 28 May.

6 *Japan Case Study* (As part of "Situation Analysis on the Effects of and Responses to COVID-19 on the Education Sector in Asia"). www.unicef.org/eap/media/9331/file/Sit%20An%20-%20Japan%20Case%20study.pdf (Accessed August 3, 2023).

7 UNESCO, Global Education Monitoring Report Summary (2020), "UNESCO's 2023 GEM Report Is About Technology in Education: A Tool on Whose Terms?", in *Inclusion and Education: All Means All*, UNESCO.

8 Ibid., p. 10.

9 www.cgdev.org/ (Accessed July 25, 2023).

10 Hares, Susannah, Rossiter, Jack and Wu, Dongyi (2023), "The State of Global Education Finance in Nine Charts: Another Update", Blog Post, June 20, www.cgdev.org/ (Accessed July 25, 2023).

5 Women Empowerment

> *Preamble: Women are the embodiment of sacrifice – most notably in the roles of wife and mother. They exert subtle affectionate authority, be it in raising children or guiding the rest of the family. Recognition of these qualities is no substitute for their empowerment, which means a lot for the future progress of families, societies, nations, and the world at large.*

5.1 Introduction

If one recognizes a problem via evidence, then only the pathways to address it could be explored. Historically, most societies felt that creation assigned distinct roles for men and women, the former receiving a superior one.[1] Significant economic progress over the last couple of centuries induced researchers to focus on the question: "for whom is this growth". Facilitated by the designing of the Gini ratio by Corrado Gini in 1912, measuring the extent of income and wealth inequality within countries and regions has become part of research and policy discourse. Over time, the quantification of inequalities on various dimensions has come to the fore, including gender inequities.

5.2 Gender Inequality Indices

Gender equality movement gained global recognition ever since it was made part of the international human rights law by the Universal Declaration of Human Rights, adopted in December 1948 by the UN General Assembly. Much had happened since, and a major milestone was the setting up of the separate agency, the UN WOMEN. Its key objectives are upholding women's human rights and ensuring that every woman and girl lives up to her full potential. The initiatives have a significant influence on the preparation and analyses of a whole host of gender inequality indicators. A few are illustrated in the rest of this section.

DOI: 10.4324/9780429059629-5

5.2.1 Gender Bias Indicator

The first ever UNDP report on gender bias[2] has data on different aspects of relevance. From Table 5.1 (pertaining to the 17 countries in focus), one can see that Japan and the United States are the only nations where close to half the population have no gender bias.[3]

The following are some of the key points from the executive summary of the UNDP Report: Without tackling biased gender social norms, achieving gender equality is not feasible. Biased gender social norms may be impeding women's economic empowerment. What can/should be done? "Education, recognition and representation can directly address biased gender social norms".[4]

5.2.2 Women Empowerment Index (WEI)[5]

The index is integral to a 2023 report prepared by UN Women and UNDP: "The paths to equal: Twin indices on women's empowerment and gender equality". WEI is a composite index, comprising five dimensions: life and good health (including bodily integrity); education, skill-building, and knowledge; labour and financial inclusion; participation in decision-making; and freedom from violence, all represented by a total of ten components.[6]

The WEI values for the focus countries are given in Table 5.2. The United States is on the top on women empowerment among the 17 countries considered. Across the world, however, there are 30 nations (mostly from Europe) above the United States. Australia is at the top with a WEI of 0.805.

5.2.3 Gender Inequality Index (GII)

GII for 2021 was accessed from the UNDP website[7] where an explanation about the index is given along with access to the data.

Table 5.1 Percentage of people with no gender bias in 17 countries, 2017–2022

The United States	49.8	India (2010–2014)	0.8
Japan	41.2	Bangladesh	0.6
Brazil	15.6	Egypt	0.5
Mexico	9.9	The Philippines	0.5
Russia	9.3	Nigeria	0.4
China	8.2	Indonesia (2010–14)	0.3
Vietnam	6.2	Pakistan	0.1
Iran	4.5	Congo, DR	NA
Ethiopia	1.2		

Table 5.2 Women Empowerment Index, 2022

Country	WEI	Country	WEI
The United States	0.752	Indonesia	0.568
China	0.664	India	0.520
Japan	0.651	Egypt	0.466
Brazil	0.637	Iran	0.454
The Philippines	0.618	Nigeria	0.444
Vietnam	0.612	Bangladesh	0.443
Mexico	0.598	Congo, DR	0.399
		Pakistan	0.337

Note: Ethiopia and Russia – NA

Table 5.3 GII 2021 across the 17 countries

Country	GII	Country	GII
Japan	0.083	Indonesia	0.444
The United States	0.179	Iran	0.459
China	0.192	India	0.490
Russia	0.203	Ethiopia	0.520
Vietnam	0.296	Bangladesh	0.530
Mexico	0.309	Pakistan	0.534
Brazil	0.390	Congo, DR	0.601
The Philippines	0.419	Nigeria	0.680
Egypt	0.443		

GII reflects gender-based disadvantage in three dimensions – reproductive health, empowerment, and the labour market – . . . It ranges from 0, where women and men fare equally, to 1, where one gender fares as poorly as possible in all measured dimensions.

As the data in Table 5.3 show, GII is the lowest in Japan with an index value of 0.08. Close to or above the half-way position are India and five more countries.

5.2.4 Global Gender Gap Index

The latest Global Gender Gap Report 2023, brought out by the World Economic Forum, provides estimates of the Global Gender Parity Index (GGGI) for 146 countries. The index is an average of four subindexes, comprising Economic Participation and Opportunity, Educational Attainment, Health and Survival, and Political Empowerment. The four sub-indexes have a few key components within each of them. (The Statistical Annex Table 8 has the full list of the components along with their weights.) The 2023 Report running into close to 400 pages is an extraordinary attempt by the World Economic

Table 5.4 GGGI 2023

Country	GGGI	Country	GGGI
The Philippines	0.791	China	0.678
Mexico	0.765	Japan	0.647
The United States	0.748	India	0.643
Brazil	0.726	Nigeria	0.637
Bangladesh	0.722	Egypt	0.626
Ethiopia	0.711	Congo, DR	0.612
Vietnam	0.711	Iran	0.575
Indonesia	0.697	Pakistan	0.575

Note: Russia – NA

Forum. It has several new sets of data specially collected by WEF and brought together at one place.

GGGI value of 1 indicates full parity between women and men. No country has achieved that unique level. Iceland in rank one came close with a score of 0.912. In the last rank (146) was Afghanistan with an index score of 0.405. As for the 17 countries in focus, the Philippines (and not the United States or Japan) is in the top position while Pakistan is at the last place.

5.2.5 Beyond Indexes

The correlation coefficient between GII and WEI was high (−0.83). It is as per expectations: where gender inequality is very low, women empowerment is very high. Between GII and GGGI, the correlation was rather low (−0.34). Between WEI and GGGI, the correlation coefficient was 0.69, implying that both have their differences and similarities.

The contribution made by the various indexes has been of great value in showcasing the prevalence of gender inequality. "The world is not on track to achieve gender equality by 2030", notes the 2022 UN SDG Report.[8] Women empowerment on all possible dimensions is the only solution. The next two sections focus on two of them: educational and political empowerments.

5.3 Educational Empowerment

It is not about literacy or primary/secondary schooling; it is about higher education. A highly educated woman would be an equal partner in all roles along with men, in addition to being the ideal "mother" nurturing the next generation. Advanced education is the key instrument of empowerment, regardless of what occupation or societal role one wishes to pursue. *The fact that women were just about 3% among the Nobel Laureates is proof of the pressing need for multivarious actions to promote women's advanced education that could propel the passion for research and innovation.*

The ground reality in respect of the 17 selected nations is reflected in the data in Table 5.5 on the percentage of women with advanced education. One can notice a clear break in the flow of the percentages after the United States, Russia, and Japan. From then on, the percentage decreases country after country. The most populous China and India have a long way to go – with around one-third and one-fifth of women with advanced education.

5.4 Political Empowerment

Going by sheer demographics, one should expect that in any national legislative body elected via free and fair elections, half the seats should be occupied by women. But what is the ground reality? The answer is in Table 5.6. Except for Mexico and Ethiopia, all other nations have less than a third of seats

Table 5.5 Women with advanced education (%), 2022

Country	%	Country	%
The United States	83	Nigeria	25
Russia	79	Brazil	24
Japan	77	Mexico	23
The Philippines	47	India	20
Egypt	46	Congo, DR	18
Iran	37	Pakistan	11
China	34	Bangladesh	10
Indonesia	34	Ethiopia	4
Vietnam	34		

Source: Social Progress Index.

Note: The data in the table is a condensed form of the original data in SPI (see Annex 1.3 for more details)

Table 5.6 Percent of women in "Parliament", 2021

Country	%	Country	%
Mexico	50	Pakistan	20
Ethiopia	43	Russia	16
Vietnam	30	Brazil	15
Egypt	28	India	14
The Philippines	28	Congo, DR	13
The United States	28	Japan	10
China	25	Iran	6
Bangladesh	21	Nigeria	4
Indonesia	21		

Source: The World Development Indicators Website (Accessed May 21, 2023).

occupied by women. Of special note is the most glaring difference between China with 25% women and India with 14% women in the highest decision-making bodies.

5.4.1 The Indian Case

Several attempts have been made since Indian Independence to ensure a certain minimum percentage of women members in all the elected bodies at the local, state, and national levels. Success has been significant in regard to local bodies (Panchayati Raj Institutions), but not at the state and national levels. For instance, in 1996, a bill proposing the reservation of one-third of seats in Parliament (Lok Sabha) did not go through. Attempts were made to pass the bill in 1998, 1999, 2002, and 2003. They did not get the required majority approval. The bill was approved in the Upper House (Rajya Sabha) in 2010 but was not taken up in the Lok Sabha (Parliament).

The Bharatiya Janata Party, in power since 2014, in its manifesto, promised 33% reservation for women. As for the progress, the following is an excerpt from *The Hindu* newspaper of July 27, 2023, about a statement made by the Law Minister in a written response to the Upper House. "The issue needs careful consideration on the basis of consensus among all political parties before a Bill for amendment in the Constitution is brought before Parliament".

Notwithstanding the many failed attempts, given below is Table 5.7 with the pertinent data from the site https://factly.in/women-mps-in-lok-sabha (accessed August 11, 2023). Women, on their own, accomplished the jump to some 15% of seats. With advances in education, they will achieve more even if there is no constitutional provision for a higher percentage.

5.4.2 IPU Efforts

There is no dearth of international organizations – whatever may be the area of concern to the humanity at large. One of them is the International Parliamentary Union. The site on its gender equality page[9] has the commendable promise: "We work to increase women's representation in parliament and empower women MPs".

Table 5.7 Women in Indian Parliament (%)

Year	%	Year	%	Year	%	Year	%
1951	4.50	1971	5.41	1989	5.48	1999	9.02
1957	4.45	1977	3.51	1991	7.30	2004	8.29
1962	6.28	1980	5.29	1996	7.37	2009	10.87
1967	5.58	1984	7.95	1998	7.92	2014	12.15

Note: Latest: 14.94% (posted on December 9, 2022, 7:15 p.m. by PIB Delhi)

The following is a notable quote from IPU's latest publication, *Women in parliament in 2022, the year in review.* "The presence of legislated gender quotas was once again decisive in 2022. Chambers with legislated quotas (or a combination of legislated quotas and voluntary party quotas) produced a significantly higher share of women than those without (30.9% versus 21.2%)" (page 14). This is a confirmation of the effectiveness of quotas, which should be considered by every nation as all important and effective.

The IPU report (pages 18–19) also showcases violence against the elected females as illustrated by the following statement pertaining to the United States: Women in politics are nearly three and a half times as likely to be targeted as men.[10] The problem can be addressed if and only if the US Congress has a mandatory 50% female representation. When they have such representation, it is almost likely that effective gun control will be implemented and violence controlled in several ways.

Has IPU a specific objective to raise the share of women in parliaments to at least a third if not half? One of the five objectives of IPU is promoting inclusive and representative parliaments: "The IPU encourages parliaments to be representative of all society, especially women, young people and marginalized populations".

IPU's good work is commendable. It is time that the august body aims for universal achievement of a 50% women's quota in parliaments and accordingly develops all its plans and programmes. There is no shortcut for women empowerment.

Notes

1 "Defined by the men in their lives, women in ancient Rome were valued mainly as wives and mothers". www.pbs.org/empires/romans/empire/women.html (Accessed August 8, 2023).

2 UNDP (2023), *2023 Gender Social Norms Index (Breaking Down Gender Biases: Shifting Social Norms Towards Gender Equality)*, United Nations Development Programme, p. 3.

3 Democratic India has little to boast; just less than 1% of the population have distanced from gender bias.

4 UNDP (2023), *2023 Gender Social Norms Index (Breaking Down Gender Biases: Shifting Social Norms Towards Gender Equality)*, United Nations Development Programme.

5 A part of the 2023 report by UN Women and UNDP, there is a Global Gender Parity Index (GGPI), which shows the status of women's achievements relative to men's in four dimensions of human development: life and good health; education, skill-building, and knowledge; labour and financial inclusion; and participation in decision-making. GGPI is available for countries grouped by level of human development, sustainable development goal regions, least developed nations, and OECD countries.

6 Component (C1): Family planning need satisfied (percentage of women aged 15–49 years); C2: adolescent birth rate (births per 1,000 women aged 15–19 years); C3: population with completed secondary education or higher, female (percentage

of women aged 25 years and older); C4: youth not in education, employment, or training, female (percentage aged 15–24 years); C5: labour force participation rate among prime-working-age individuals who are living in a household comprising a couple and at least one child under age six years, female (percentage aged 25–54 years); C6: account ownership at a financial institution or with a mobile-money-service provider, female (percentage of population 15 years and older); C7: percentage of females in parliament; C8: percentage of females in local governments; C9: percentage of females in managerial positions; *and* C10: percentage of females aged 15–49 years subjected to sexual violence in the past 12 months.

7 https://hdr.undp.org/data-center/thematic-composite-indices/gender-inequality-index (Accessed August 5, 2023).

8 United Nations (2022), *The Sustainable Development Goals Report 2022*, United Nations, p. 36.

9 www.ipu.org/impact/gender-equality (Accessed August 11, 2023).

10 The following substantiates the statement. In 2022, at least one female member of Congress was forced to change her sleeping location after receiving threats. Other incidents include: an armed assailant breaking into the home of Speaker Nancy Pelosi and injuring her husband who was alone; and other women Congress members' stories of being followed by armed stalkers, inundated with online death threats, and having their offices vandalized.

6 Hope for the Future

> *The numerous global indexes and reports have achieved the objective of showcasing the problems and suggesting possible solutions. The hope for the future rests on the idea that global institutions take direct action via full cooperation and coordination with national and local governments.*

6.1 About the UN System

Based on the information at www.un.org/en/about-us/un-system,[1] there are a total of 38 agencies under the UN system. Some have done exemplary humanitarian work as summarized in the following sub-section.

6.1.1 Great Successes

Of special significance to the global community's welfare and progress over the post-war period were some of the key UN agencies. The United Nations itself is a great asset to the world. Its General Assembly is like a world parliament to debate and discuss issues of concern for the humanity at large as well as for the people of specific countries.

Among the UN system agencies, apart from the IMF and the World Bank, most popular in terms of impact and contributions are the following, in particular: Food and Agriculture Organization; International Civil Aviation Organization; International Maritime Organization; International Telecommunication Union; UN Educational, Scientific and Cultural Organization; Universal Postal Union; World Health Organization; World Intellectual Property Organization; World Meteorological Organization; UN Women, United Nations Framework Convention on Climate Change; and the World Trade Organization.

DOI: 10.4324/9780429059629-6

6.1.2 Learning from UNIDIR

The United Nations Institute for Disarmament Research (UNIDIR) website has the following introductory statement: "With over 40 years of experience, UNIDIR . . . conducts independent research on disarmament and related problems; particularly international security issues".[2]

The research output runs into more than 100 publications. Here is a short list of the latest titles: **Revitalizing the conference on disarmament: workshop report; A lexicon for outer space security; **Menzingen verification experiment: verifying the absence of nuclear weapons in the field; **Narratives of the Middle East WMD-free zone: drivers, themes and historical accounts; **Addressing chemical and biological weapons challenges through the Middle East weapons of mass destruction-free zone: workshop report; *and* **Addressing weapons in conflict-related sexual violence: the arms control and disarmament toolbox.

The intellectuals have done their best to demonstrate the evil called violence at the global level propelled by the arms race. What is perhaps not researched is why leaders of nations fall into the defence spending trap, and why they welcome the fighting spirit even when there is no pressing need for a fight. *It is indeed distressing that UN and its system could not prevent the Ukraine war, not to mention the routine border skirmishes that happen so often.*

6.1.3 Time for UN Reform

The good news is that the UN has taken some serious steps in regard to its reform. There is a website https://reform.un.org/ (accessed August 23, 2023) which is all about UN reform. Here is an important quote from the opening page of the site: "The overarching goals of the reform are to prioritize prevention and sustaining peace; . . . and move towards a single, integrated peace and security pillar".

May be, the "ageing" UN system needs a fresh evaluation and rejuvenation. Annex 7 has a few indicative ideas for consideration about the future of the UN system. The ideas translate into moving from the present 38 agencies to 22. The Annex also has a tabulation on the present headquarters locations of the 38 agencies. Except for 2 in Kenya and 1 in Jordan, remaining 35 are in developed countries, with the largest number (12) in Geneva. Relocation of some of the headquarters to developing countries should be considered.

Then there is the perennial issue of the reform of the Security Council: the question of equitable representation on, and increase in, the membership of the Security Council and other matters related to the Council. The topic was discussed at several of the meetings of the General Assembly over the years. As of August 25, 2023, it is expected that the matter will be taken up once again at the 78th session of the UN General Assembly opening on Tuesday,

September 5, 2023, with the high-level debates taking place from September 19, 2023 through September 29.

6.2 Food for All: Top Priority

Food, the primary necessity for survival, is all important. In the background of economic growth and development since the Industrial Revolution, organizations of the UN system did their best to ensure minimal hunger and starvation.

To ensure that none of the present-day 8 billion world residents will ever suffer from the lack of food, a fresh initiative is needed. Table 6.1 concerning the 17 countries in focus has pertinent data on net food trade and food security.

For each country, the per capita *food trade* deficit/surplus (in $) was computed on the basis of the total food trade deficit in 2020 and the population as of 2021. Also given for each country were the Global Food Security Index (GFSI)[3] original ranks (in parentheses) and the rank within the 17 countries. Food affordability, availability, quality and safety, and sustainability and adaptation were represented by unique indicators in the making of GFSI.

6.2.1 Two Concerns

The top three countries in terms of GFSI ranks are Japan, the United States, and China. Yet, they had food trade deficits per capita of $400, $80, and $81, respectively. In addition, there are seven more nations with deficits.

One concern is that rich nations can afford to pay and obtain essential food items from any nation ready to sell. That money power "might" create pockets

Table 6.1 Per capita Net Food Trade ($) and Global Food Security (Index) Rank

Country and GFSI Original Rank[*]	2020–2021 per capita trade ($)	GFSI Rank within 17	Country and GFSI Original Rank[*]	2020–2021 per capita trade ($)	GFSI Rank within 17
Japan (6)	−400	1	The Philippines (67)	−43	8
The United States (13)	−80	2	India (68)	10	9
China (25)	−81	3	Egypt (77)	−78	10
Mexico (43)	122	4	Bangladesh (80)	−47	11
Russia (43)	5	4	Pakistan (84)	−12	12
Vietnam (46)	86	5	Ethiopia (100)	0	13
Brazil (51)	296	6	Congo, DR (104)	−6	14
Indonesia (63)	70	7	Nigeria (107)	−27	15
			Iran	−44	NA

For data sources and more details, see Table 9 of the Statistical Annex.

[*] Rank out of a total of 113 nations. Finland is at rank 1 and Syria at 113.

of hunger in the selling country. The second concern is regarding countries that do not produce enough food and do not have the money power to buy the food from rest of the world. There is no easy solution for balancing food production and consumption across every country.[4] It must be a global balancing act supervised effectively by a global agency.

6.2.2 *International Initiatives*[5]

Of the United Nations' 17 Sustainable Development Goals, Goal 2 is to achieve zero hunger by 2030. There is a 2022 Report entitled "State of Food Security and Nutrition in the World".[6] Here is an excerpt from its Foreword: "This report repeatedly highlights the intensification of these major drivers of food insecurity and malnutrition: conflict, climate extremes and economic shocks, combined with growing inequalities" (p. vi).

In direct reference to the SDG Goal 2, the following is a statement from the Report (p. xiv): "Projections are that nearly 670 million people will still be facing hunger in 2030 - 8 percent of the world population, . . . same as in 2015 when the 2030 Agenda was launched". Here is a key recommendation (p. xxiii):

[G]overnments start rethinking how they can reallocate their existing public budgets to make them more cost-effective and efficient in reducing the cost of nutritious foods and increasing the availability and affordability of healthy diets, with sustainability and leaving no one behind.

There are several UN organizations working for ensuring food security globally. The World Food Programme (WFP) provides food assistance to countries in need and responds to emergencies. "The World Bank Group works with partners to improve food security and build a food system that can feed everyone, everywhere, every day".[7] Achieving food security for all is the core goal of the FAO. The International Fund for Agricultural Development (IFAD) focusses on rural poverty reduction.

6.2.3 *Initiative for the Future*

Here is what may seem like a daydream for now: the entire world food stock will be collected and managed by a global entity, with regional, national, and sub-national outfits helping with the complex dimensions of raising output and distribution as per need. All the concerned international organizations should create an expert panel to draft the design of a global food security system. Nations contribute food and/or funds. Just one global agency (could be named the Global Food Security Agency) takes responsibility for all activities now performed by FAO, IFAD, and WFP and takes on the added role of ensuring global food security. Since the new agency has roles linked to production and distribution, its regional, national, and local branches will have a lot of work to do in collaborating with farmers at the ground level and going all the way to government departments and ministries.

6.3 Addressing Visible Inequalities

A monumental contribution of the United Nations was the declaration of the Sustainable Development Goals. The SDGs were approved in 2015 by the UN General Assembly. The 17 interlinked global goals along with 169 targets within them[8] are all to be achieved by 2030.

> Regarding addressing visible inequalities, *of special importance are the SDGs 3, 4, and 5: good health, quality education, and gender equality respectively.* Directly or indirectly, these objectives (especially the first two) need the strong foundation of appropriate housing facilities.

The target is not erasing income and wealth inequalities by any means to showcase visible equality. The target is to harvest latent human values to produce equal access to essential housing, best education, and good health care. In addition, there needs to be a focus on gender equality. *Development in true sense should be taken as the lowest degree of visible inequalities.*

6.3.1 Visible Inequalities

- Here is a four-point summary of visible inequalities. First, private housing estates and spacious bungalows are kept separate from the dwellings of the low-income groups. Second, low-income families lose all their "wealth" when they get top medical treatment at a corporate hospital. Third, there are no general provisions such as merit-based quotas for children from the low-income families to get admission in top private schools. Fourth, there is widespread practice of male supremacy and dominance with little or no concern for gender equality. All these together manifest as highly visible inequalities.

6.3.2 The Hope

Bess (2022)[9] identifies four greatest challenges facing the humanity at large: climate change, nukes, pandemics, and artificial intelligence. He suggests a transformation of the United Nations to be an effective organization to propose and coordinate "global solutions to humanity's problems".

UN-Habitat could be the one global agency to ensure housing for all. *WHO* ensures health care for every human.[10] UNESCO orchestrates a common education programme from primary through higher secondary with one global exam and grading system. UN-Women plans and supervises national and local initiatives on gender equality.

6.4 The Climate Change Challenge

For tackling the very important "Climate Challenge", the 40-page "Summary for Policy Makers"[11] by a distinguished group of experts documented in the 2021 publication has the following important observations.

- "It is unequivocal that human influence has warmed the atmosphere, ocean, and land. Widespread and rapid changes in the atmosphere, ocean, cryosphere, and biosphere have occurred" (Page 4 of the Summary for Policy Makers). "Human influence has warmed the climate at a rate that is unprecedented in at least the last 2000 years (Page 6). "Global warming of 1.5°C and 2°C will be exceeded during the 21st century unless deep reductions in CO_2 and other greenhouse gas emissions occur in the coming decades" (Page 14).

Enough has been said on the problem. It is time for tough actions. With respect to every sector contributing to global warming, specific actions need to be designed and firmly implemented. Here is one example: levying a very heavy sales tax on private motor cars and subsidizing and encouraging public transport – *indeed, that transportation transformation could also promote visibility of equality.*

Notes

1 (Accessed April 20, 2023). See also Annex 6.
2 https://unidir.org/about (Accessed August 20, 2023).
3 See the Global Food Security Index 2022, Developed by Economist Impact and supported by Corteva Agriscience.
4 Perhaps it is a great world wonder that there is no natural law insisting on food security before nation formation.
5 Based on www.un.org/en/global-issues/food (Accessed August 18, 2023).
6 FAO, IFAD, UNICEF, WFP and WHO (2022), *The State of Food Security and Nutrition in the World 2022: Repurposing Food and Agricultural Policies to Make Healthy Diets More Affordable*, FAO.
7 Source: www.un.org/en/global-issues/food (Accessed August 18, 2023).
8 Details are in Annex 1.
9 Bess, Michael D. (2022), *Planet in Peril: Humanity's Four Greatest Challenges and How We Can Overcome Them*, Cambridge University Press.
10 According to the Stockholm International Peace Research Institute, global military expenditure rose by 3.7 per cent in real terms in 2022, to reach a record high of

$2,240 billion. With world population at 8 billion, the military expense works out to $280 per person. It could very well fund a global health care initiative, if only there is an all-nations agreement to stop all military spending effective from an agreed date well before 2030.

11 Intergovernmental Panel on Climate Change (2021), *Climate Change 2021: The Physical Science Basis, Summary for Policy Makers*, Working Group I Contribution to the Sixth Assessment Report, IPCC.

Two Valuable Quotes

In politics we will be recognizing the principle of one man one vote and one vote one value. In our social and economic life, we shall, by reason of our social and economic structure, continue to deny the principle of one man one value. How long shall we continue to live this life of contradictions? How long shall we continue to deny equality in our social and economic life?

– B R Ambedkar

Everyone should respect all others as one's own kin, having the same Divine Spark, and the same Divine Nature. Then, there will be effective production, economic consumption, and equitable distribution, resulting in peace and promotion of love. Now, love based on the Innate Divinity is absent and so, there is exploitation, deceit, greed, and cruelty.

– Bhagawan Sri Sathya Sai in His Discourse on April 1, 1975

DOI: 10.4324/9780429059629-7

References

Alfani, Guido (2021), "Economic Inequality in Pre-Industrial Times: Europe and Beyond", *Journal of Economic Literature*, 59(1), 3–44.

Baker, Emma and Bentley, Rebecca (Eds.) (2023), "Housing, Inequality, and Health", *International Journal of Housing Policy*, 23(2), Special Issue.

Bess, Michael D. (2022), *Planet in Peril: Humanity's Four Greatest Challenges and How We Can Overcome Them*, Cambridge University Press.

Bhaumik, Mani (2005, 2017), *Code Name God, the Spiritual Odyssey of a Man of Science*, Penguin Random House India.

Blanchard, Olivier and Rodrik, Dani (Eds.) (2021), *Combating Inequality: Rethinking Government's Role*, The MIT Press.

Booth, Anne (2019), *Living Standards in Southeast Asia, Changes Over the Long Twentieth Century, 1900–2015*, Amsterdam University Press.

Chen, Cui and Liu, Mao (2023), "Achievements and Challenges of the Healthcare System in China", *Cureus*, 15(5), May 15.

Commonwealth Fund Commission on a National Public Health System (2022), *Meeting America's Public Health Challenge: Recommendations for Building a National Public Health System That Addresses Ongoing and Future Health Crises, Advances Equity, and Earns Trust*, The Commonwealth Fund.

Dougherty, Conor (2021), *Golden Gates: The Housing Crisis and a Reckoning for the American Dream*, Penguin Books.

FAO, IFAD, UNICEF, WFP and WHO (2022), *The State of Food Security and Nutrition in the World 2022 (Repurposing Food and Agricultural Policies to Make Healthy Diets More Affordable)*, FAO.

Government of NCT of Delhi, Directorate of Economics & Statistics (2020), *Report on Socio-Economic Profile of Residents of Delhi (Part 1: Households Characteristics)*, Government of NCT of Delhi, Directorate of Economics & Statistics, March.

Government of NCT of Delhi, Directorate of Economics & Statistics (2021), *Drinking Water, Sanitation, Hygiene and Housing Condition in Delhi, Based on the State Sample of the National Sample Survey, July 2018 – December 2018*, Government of NCT of Delhi, Directorate of Economics & Statistics, September.

Gavari-Starkie, Elisa, Casado-Claro, María-Francisca and Navarro-González, Inmaculada (2021), "The Japanese Educational System as an International Model for Urban Resilience", *International Journal of Environmental Research and Public Health*, 18(11), 5794, 28 May.

Grusky, David B. and Hill, Jasmine (Eds.) (2018), *Inequality in the 21st Century, a Reader*, Westview Press.

Hares, Susannah, Rossiter, Jack and Wu, Dongyi (2023), "The State of Global Education Finance in Nine Charts: Another Update", Blog Post, June 20, www.cgdev.org/ (Accessed July 25, 2023).

Huang, Tianlei (2023), *Why China's Housing Policies Have Failed*, Working Papers 23–25, Peterson Institute for International Economics.

Intergovernmental Panel on Climate Change (2021), *Climate Change 2021: The Physical Science Basis, Summary for Policy Makers*, Working Group I Contribution to the Sixth Assessment Report, IPCC.

Korver-Glenn, Elizabeth, Locklear, Sofia, Howell, Junia and Whitehead, Ellen (2023), "Displaced and Unsafe: The Legacy of Settler-Colonial Racial Capitalism in the U.S. Rental Market", *Journal of Race, Ethnicity, and the City*, 1–22.

Kondo, Tatsuya and MEJ Four-Dimensional Health Innovation Group (2022), "Report on the Nature, Characteristics, and Outcomes of the Japanese Healthcare System", *Global Health & Medicine*, 4(1), 37–44, February 28.

Lalueza-Fox, Carles (2022), *Inequality: A Genetic History*, The MIT Press.

Li, Chunling and Fan, Yiming (2020), "Housing Wealth Inequality in Urban China: The Transition from Welfare Allocation to Market Differentiation", *The Journal of Chinese Sociology*, 7, Article Number 16.

Norman, Donald A. (2023), *Design for a Better World: Meaningful, Sustainable, Humanity Centered*, The MIT Press.

Sakamoto, Haruka, et al. (2018), *Japan Health System Review*, vol. 8, no. 1, World Health Organization, Regional Office for South-East Asia.

Selvaraj, S., Karan, K.A., Srivastava, Swati, Bhan, Nandita and Mukhopadhyay, Indranil (2022), *India Health System Review*, World Health Organization, Regional Office for South-East Asia.

Scheidel, Walter (2017), *The Great Leveler: Violence and the History of Inequality from Stone Age to the Twenty-First Century*, Princeton University Press.

Schwartz, Alex F. (2021), *Housing Policy in the United States*, Routledge.

Thakur, Dinesh Singh, and Prashant, Reddy (2022), *The Truth Pill: The Myth of Drug Regulation in India*, Simon & Schuster.

UNDP (2023), *2023 Gender Social Norms Index (Breaking Down Gender Biases: Shifting Social Norms Towards Gender Equality)*, United Nations Development Programme.

UNESCO, Global Education Monitoring Report Summary (2020), "UNESCO's 2023 GEM Report Is About Technology in Education: A Tool on Whose Terms?", in *Inclusion and Education: All Means All*, UNESCO.

United Nations (2020), *World Social Report 2020: Inequality in a Rapidly Changing World*, The United Nations Department of Economic and Social Affairs.

United Nations (2022), *The Sustainable Development Goals Report 2022*, United Nations.

Winegarden, Wayne, et al. (2021), *No Way Home: The Crisis of Homelessness and How to Fix It with Intelligence and Humanity*, Encounter Books.

Yamanaka, Shinichi and Suzuki, Kan Hiroshi (2020), "Japanese Education Reform Towards Twenty-First Century Education", in Reimers, Fernando M. (Ed.) *Audacious Education Purposes*, Springer, pp. 81–103.

Yang, Lixiong (2018), *The Social Assistance Reform in China: Towards a Fair and Inclusive Social Safety Net*, Paper for the Conference on "Addressing Inequalities and Challenges to Social Inclusion Through Fiscal, Wage and Social Protection Policies", United Nations, June 25–27.

Zhu, Yishan, et al. (2022), "How Do Chinese People Perceive Their Healthcare System? Trends and Determinants of Public Satisfaction and Perceived Fairness, 2006–2019", *BMC Health Services Research*, 22.

Annexes

Annex 1

The Sustainable Development Goals

Origin and Background

The Sustainable Development Goals refer to a collection of 17 interlinked global goals designed to be a "blueprint to achieve a better and more sustainable future for all". The goals were worked out in 2015 by the United Nations General Assembly.[1] The target date for achievement was set as 2030.

The 17 SDGs and 169 Targets

The following is the list of goals and numbers of targets (in parenthesis) available on *https://sdgs.un.org/goals* (accessed on April 30, 2023).

1: No Poverty **(7)**	*7: Affordable and Clean Energy* **(5)**	*13: Climate Action* **(5)**
2: Zero Hunger **(8)**	*8: Decent Work and Economic Growth* **(12)**	*14: Life Below Water* **(10)**
3: Good Health and Well-Being **(13)**	*9: Industry, Innovation, and Infrastructure Growth* **(8)**	*15: Life on Land* **(12)**
4: Quality Education **(10)**	*10: Reduced Inequality* **(10)**	*16: Peace- and Justice- Strong Institutions* **(12)**
5: Gender Equality **(9)**	*11: Sustainable Cities and Communities* **(10)**	*17: Partnerships to Achieve the Goals* **(19)**
6: Clean Water and Sanitation **(8)**	*12: Responsible Consumption and Production* **(11)**	

Great Hope

A total understanding of the targets, full commitment of all the nations of the globe, and further advancement of the targets to the most achievable levels in practice – these could help accomplish a significant narrowing of cross-country welfare differences. With regard to visible inequalities, goals 3, 4, and 5 (respectively good health, quality education, and gender equality) are especially important. These goals, targets, and information on achievements from the latest UN progress report[2] are noted and reviewed in the relevant chapters.

Annex 2

Social and Economic Indicators Compiled by the United Nations, the World Bank, and IISS

UN Statistics

For authentic data across countries, one key source is the site: https://unstats.un.org/unsd/demographic/products/socind/ (accessed April 6, 2023): "Social indicators covering a wide range of subject-matter fields are compiled by the Statistics Division, Department of Economic and Social Affairs of the United Nations Secretariat, from many national and international sources".

The indicators are given in five groups: population, health, housing, education, and work. Population size, growth, composition, and distribution are covered under the first group. Under health, the following groups of indicators are provided: life expectancy, maternal mortality and infant mortality, childbearing, contraceptive prevalence, and HIV/AIDS.

Average number of persons per room by urban/rural area, population distribution (%) by urban/rural area, annual rate of population change (%) by urban/rural area, improved drinking water coverage (%) by urban/rural area, and improved sanitation coverage (%) by urban/rural area are provided under the category of housing indicators.

Adult (15+) literacy rate, by sex; youth (15–24) literacy rate, by sex; primary net enrolment ratio, by sex; girl's share of primary enrolment; secondary net enrolment ratio, by sex; girl's share of secondary enrolment; tertiary gross enrolment ratio, by sex; women's share of tertiary enrolment; and school life expectancy (primary to tertiary education) by sex – these are the indicators covered under education.

Under "work", nine indicators are given under four categories: income and economic activity, part-time employment, distribution of labour force by status in employment, and adult unemployment.

While some of the indicators at the maximum possible level could imply visible equality, there are no direct indicators of visibility of equality.

World Development Indicators

The site (*https://wdi.worldbank.org/tables*, accessed May 31, 2023) provides a large number of indicators grouped under the following heads: WORLD VIEW, POVERTY AND SHARED PROSPERITY, PEOPLE, ENVIRONMENT, ECONOMY, STATES AND MARKETS, GLOBAL LINKS, and COUNTRY PROFILES. Again, some of the indicators could imply visible equality, and these are covered in the following chapters.

Erasmus University Rotterdam's Indices of Social Development

The ISD information given next is based on a 2011 presentation by Ellen Webbink of the International Institute of Social Studies, Erasmus University Rotterdam. the Netherlands.

The Six Indices of Social Development were identified as follows: Civic Activism (strength of civil society – levels of civic activism and access to information); Interpersonal Safety and Trust (norms of nonviolence between persons in society); Inter-group Cohesion (relations of trust and cohesion between defined ethnic, religious, or linguistic identity groups); Clubs and Associations (relations of trust and cohesion within local communities); Gender Equity (non-discrimination against women); *and* Inclusion of Minorities (Non-exclusion of social minorities & indigenous peoples).

Based on the information on *https://isd.iss.nl/data-access/* (accessed May 26, 2023), ISD variables number a whopping total of **275** and are distributed as follows: **43** relating to *civic activism* such as attend political protest, sign petition, join boycott, radios per capita, newspapers per capita, percentage of people reading newspaper last week, percentage watching TV reports last week, and international NGO membership relative to population; **65** pertaining to *clubs and associations*, comprising indicators such as percentages: those considering family as important, friends important, trusting neighbourhood, are active members of political parties, are active members of labour unions, spending time with relatives once a week or more, and helping someone find a job last year; **44** on *gender equality* such as female–male tertiary enrolment ratio, female administrators' ratio, discrimination of women in family law, women in parliament, women's economic rights, women's social rights, and percentage of managers who think men are better managers; **49** on *inclusion of minorities* that include variables such as uneven economic development along groups (rating), ethnic tension (rating), not as neighbours – different race, not as neighbours – different religion, religious tension (rating), educational disparity – different ethnic groups, **18** on *inter-group cohesion* which comprise indicators such as deaths in conflict (rating), ryots per capita, terrorism risk (rating), guerrilla attacks per capita, riots per capita, and minority rebellion score; *and* **56** on *interpersonal safety and trust* indicators such as car theft rate, percentage feeling safe in their area in the night, robberies in neighbourhood, sex-exploitation, rating of social distrust, homicide rate, percentage experiencing theft in the last five years, percentage of owners having car vandalism in the last five years, percentage of people suffering break-in last five years, percentage of women facing sexual harassment in the last five years, and percentage not trusting their neighbourhood.

Despite the uniqueness and innovative nature of the inclusion of so many indicators, there is no comprehensive set of indicators of visible equality. The exception is a few of the 44 gender equality indicators – more on this is taken up in Chapter 5.

Annex 3

A Note on the Social Progress Index

Defining Social Progress

The Social Progress Initiative defines social progress as

> the capacity of a society to meet the basic human needs of its citizens, establish the building blocks that allow citizens and communities to enhance and sustain the quality of their lives, and create the conditions for all individuals to reach their full potential.

Three dimensions of social progress are identified as follows: *basic human needs, foundations of well-being, and opportunities.* Four components are identified under these three dimensions for constructing the social progress index.

Dimensions of Social Progress

Capacity to meet basic needs: this dimension measures the capacity of a nation to meet basic human needs like nutrition, basic health care, sanitation, availability of clean and safe drinking water, shelter, and personal safety.

Building blocks to sustain and enhance well-being: this dimension pertains to access to quality education (basic knowledge), access to information and communication facilities, health and wellness, and environmental quality.

Opportunities to achieve full potential: this dimension measures personal rights, personal freedom and choice, inclusiveness, and access to advanced education.

Twelve Components and 60 Indicators

- *Nutrition and Basic Medical Care:* 1. infectious diseases, 2. child mortality rate, 3. child stunting, 4. maternal mortality rate, 5. undernourishment, 6. diet low in fruits and vegetables.
- *Water and Sanitation:* 7. access to improved sanitation; 8. access to an improved water source; 9. unsafe water, sanitation, and hygiene; 10. satisfaction with water quality.
- *Housing Facilities:* 11. household air pollution, 12. dissatisfaction with housing affordability, 13. access to electricity, 14. usage of clean fuels and technology for cooking.
- *Personal Safety:* 15. interpersonal violence, 16. transportation-related injuries, 17. political killings and torture, 18. intimate partner violence, 19. money stolen.
- *Access to the Basic Knowledge:* 20. population with no schooling, 21. equal access to quality education, 22. primary school enrolment, 23. secondary school attainment 24. gender parity in secondary attainment.
- *Access to Information and Communications:* 25. access to online governance, 26. number of internet users, 27. mobile telephone subscriptions, 28. alternative sources of information index.
- *Foundations of Well-being:* 29. life expectancy at 60 years of age, 30. premature deaths from non-communicable diseases, 31. equal access to quality healthcare, 32. access to essential health services, 33. satisfaction with the availability of quality healthcare.
- *Environmental Quality:* 34. outdoor air pollution, 35. lead exposure, 36. particulate matter pollution, 37. species protection.
- *Personal Rights:* 38. access to justice, 39. freedom of religion, 40. political rights, 41. property rights for women, 42. freedom of peaceful assembly, 43. freedom of discussion.
- *Personal Freedom and Choice:* 44. satisfied demand for contraception; 45. perception of corruption; 46. early marriage; 47. youth not in education, employment, or training; 48. vulnerable employment; 49. freedom of domestic movement.
- *Inclusiveness:* 50. equal protection index, 51.equal access index, 52. power distributed by sexual orientation, 53. access to public services distributed by social group, 54. acceptance of gays and lesbians, 55. discrimination and violence against minorities.
- *Access to Advanced Education:* 56. citable documents, 57. academic freedom, 58. women with advanced education, 59. expected years of tertiary schooling, 60. quality weighted universities.

Index Construction

Equal weightage is assigned to all the components and dimensions. To make comparisons easier, the components, dimensions, and overall performance scores are scaled from 0 to 100.

Top Performers among the Selected 28 Nations

The following table provides the SPI values and the 2022 ranks of the 28 selected nations. Seven countries achieved top ranks and also indicator values in the 80–90 range. It is clear that not every nation can make it to the best index values; most notable are the most populous China and India which are in the 60–65 range.

SPI 2011 and 2022 for the Selected 28 Countries

Country	2011	2022	Country	2011	2022
Germany	87.60	88.72	Indonesia	59.24	66.67
Japan	85.46	88.19	Turkey	65.08	66.59
Korea, Rep.	83.36	86.47	**China**	**57.05**	**65.74**
The United Kingdom	86.41	86.13	Iran	58.10	63.72
France	84.71	86.07	**India**	**51.70**	**60.19**
Italy	81.38	85.23	Egypt	53.77	58.73
The United States	84.59	84.65	Kenya	49.64	57.96
Russia	67.36	71.99	Bangladesh	47.81	56.06
Brazil	70.68	71.26	Tanzania	46.54	54.87
Mexico	66.41	70.84	Nigeria	45.56	52.97
South Africa	62.09	69.95	Myanmar	43.03	51.46
Thailand	66.96	69.80	Pakistan	45.39	51.32
Vietnam	61.37	68.18	Ethiopia	37.55	47.43
The Philippines	63.16	67.46	Congo, DR	33.73	42.70

Concluding Notes

SPI is a commendable initiative going far beyond GDP per capita and allied measures. The chapters on housing, health, and education of this book have benefitted immensely from the SPI initiative in the three areas.

Annex 4

Income and Wealth Inequality: Trends and Policy Perspectives

The top 20 articles on income and wealth inequality (listed next) selected by six luminaries[3] from those published in the first 100 years of *The American Economic Review* were the subject of an essay in AER's February 2011 issue.

Hundred Years of AER: The Top 20 Articles

Year	Year and Title (Arranged in Alphabetical order of Principal Author)
1972	Alchian, Armen A., and Harold Demsetz: *Production, Information Costs*, and *Economic Organization*
1963	Arrow, Kenneth J: *Uncertainty and the Welfare Economics of Medical Care*
1928	Cobb, Charles W., and Paul H. Douglas: *A Theory of Production*
1980	Deaton, Angus S., and John Muellbauer: *An Almost Ideal Demand System*
1965	Diamond, Peter A: *National Debt in a Neoclassical Growth Model*
1971	Diamond, Peter A., and James A. Mirrlees: *Optimal Taxation and Public Production I: Production Efficiency*
1977	Dixit, Avinash K., and Joseph E. Stiglitz *Monopolistic Competition and Optimum Product Diversity*
1968	Friedman, Milton: *The Role of Monetary Policy*
1980	Grossman, Sanford J., and Joseph E. Stiglitz: *On the Impossibility of Informationally Efficient Markets*
1970	Harris, John R., and Michael P. Todaro: *Migration, Unemployment and Development: A Two-Sector Analysis*
1945	Hayek, RA: *The Use of Knowledge in Society*
1963	Jorgenson, Dale W: *Capital Theory and Investment Behavior*
1974	Krueger, Anne: *The Political Economy of the Rent-Seeking Society*
1980	Krugman, Paul: *Scale Economies, Product Differentiation, and the Pattern of Trade*
1955	Kuznets, Simon: Economic Growth and Income Inequality
1973	Lucas, Robert E., Jr: *Some International Evidence on Output-Inflation Trade-offs*
1958	Modigliani, Franco, and Merton H. Miller: *The Cost of Capital, Corporation Finance and the Theory of Investment*
1961	Mundell, Robert A: *A Theory of Optimum Currency Areas*
1973	Ross, Stephen A: *The Economic Theory of Agency: The Principal's Problem*
1981	Shiller, Robert J: *Do Stock Prices Move Too Much to Be Justified by Subsequent Changes in Dividends*

The Kuznets Article in Top 20

One of the top 20 articles was the 1955 article of Simon Kuznets that helped in propagating the Kuznets hypothesis. In brief, the hypothesis postulates that over a long period of economic growth, income inequality first increases and then declines. His article promoted a high volume of empirical research on economic growth and income inequality.

The Alfani Article

Despite the extreme difficulty of tracking historical indicators of income and wealth inequality, several laudable attempts have been made by reputed researchers. Among the most recent was Guido Alfani's 2021 article.[4] He investigated the historical trends in wealth and income inequality over a fairly long period of time (1300–2010). Here is an implication of the historical trends: "history does not support the view of a 'spontaneous' tendency for inequality to decline" (p. 37).

The paper's concluding statement is on policy:

> The long-run, historical perspective attempted here, then, also offers us a clear policy implication . . . : if we want a less unequal society, then we have to act to create it, as it seems unlikely that inequality will begin to decline on its own.

(Alfani, page 40)

Global Snapshot

Based on the data in the *World Inequality Report 2022*, Tables A4.1 and A4.2 were prepared.[5]

Table A4.1 Income Inequality

Region	Bottom 50%	Middle 40%	Top 10%
Europe	19%	45%	36%
South & SE Asia	12%	33%	55%
East Asia	14%	43%	43%
North America	13%	41%	46%
Sub-Saharan Africa	9%	35%	56%
Russia & Central Asia	15%	39%	47%
Middle East & North Africa	9%	33%	58%
Latin America	10%	34%	55%

Source: 2022 World Inequality Report.

Table A4.2 Wealth Inequality

Region	Bottom 50%	Middle 40%	Top 10%
Europe	4%	37%	59%
South & SE Asia	5%	28%	67%
East Asia	5%	26%	69%
North America	2%	28%	70%
Sub-Saharan Africa	1%	26%	73%
Russia & Central Asia	3%	24%	73%
Middle East & North Africa	1%	22%	77%
Latin America	1%	22%	77%

Source: 2022 World Inequality Report.

A glaring comparative is between the top 10% shares in income and wealth, with the wealth share being higher than the income share across all regions. The difference is maximum at 26 percentage points in East Asia (which includes China) and in Russia and Central Asia (where Russia is the key player). Europe stands for the lowest income and wealth shares of the top 10%. There, even though industry and economic activity are fostered by private enterprises, people at large are considerate in ensuring the welfare of each other.[6]

Gini Ratios[7] Across 106 Nations

Table A4.3 has the summary picture of the cross-country Gini ratios for incomes for years close to 2020.[8] The diversity across the nations is so evident that none could ever think of formulating one theory that could fit all. Inequality is neither region-specific nor ethnicity-specific. It is pervasive.

Inter-correlations

In addition to the Net Income Gini reported in the earlier table, the original data set has estimates on the following variables also: *wealth Gini, daily median income, and poverty rate.* Since as many as 106 nations are covered, it

Table A4.3 Cross-country Gini, For Years Close to 2020 (Major "industrialized" countries are in italics)

Gini	Countries in the Range [No.]
>0.5	S. Africa, Namibia, Sri Lanka, China (4)
0.45–0.5	Zambia, Lesotho, Colombia, Honduras, the Philippines, India, Egypt, Panama, Chile, Mexico, Costa Rica, Indonesia, Peru, Paraguay, Brazil, Tajikistan, Dominican Republic [17]
0.4–0.45	Guatemala, Rwanda, Russia, Thailand, Bolivia, Nicaragua, Malaysia, Tanzania, Vietnam, Kenya, Laos, Georgia, Jordan [13]
0.38–0.4	Mozambique, Singapore, Zimbabwe, Cameroon, Turkey, Nepal, Bangladesh, Nigeria, El Salvador, Iran, Albania, Argentina, Chad, Ghana, Mongolia, *the United States,* Uganda [17]
0.34–0.38	Malawi, Madagascar, Uruguay, Israel, Cambodia, Latvia, Pakistan, Armenia, Morocco, Portugal, Senegal, Estonia, *Spain,* Lithuania, Kyrgyzstan, Serbia, Bulgaria, Moldova [18]
0.3–0.34	Tunisia, *Italy, Greece, Australia, Romania, the United Kingdom, New Zealand,* Mali, Algeria, Poland, Sierra Leone, Burundi, *Canada,* South Korea, Mauritania, *Ireland, France, Japan* [18]
0.24–0.3	Croatia, *Switzerland, Germany,* Kazakhstan, Hungary, Azerbaijan, *Luxembourg, Austria, the Netherlands,* Ukraine, Slovakia, Slovenia, *Belgium, Sweden, Finland,* Czech Republic, *Denmark, Norway, Iceland* [19]

Table A4.4 Correlation between Income Gini and Three Other Variables

	Across 106 countries	*31 low-income nations*
Wealth Gini	0.26	0.34
Median income	**−0.60**	0.27
Poverty rate	0.27	−0.25

is enlightening to work out the inter-correlations between income Gini, wealth Gini, median income, and poverty rate. Table A4.4 has the correlation coefficients for all the countries and 31 low-income countries.

Every country in the world has the elements of capitalism and socialism in different and changing proportions. Hence, one does not expect income and wealth inequalities to be fully related. For all the nations taken together, daily median income and net income Gini are negatively correlated, with the correlation coefficient being high. Thus, as economies become more and more advanced, there is hope for income inequality to decline. That poverty reduction has priority regardless of income inequality is implied by the very low correlation between the two.

Not to Forget the Data Issues

It is certainly a great achievement that we have Gini ratios for 106 nations. However, it is too much to assume that the across countries' data are of the same quality.

WIR Policy Focus

It is not out of place to appreciate the lead author Lucas Chancel of the Paris School of Economics for bringing out such an exemplary reader-friendly WIR 2022. The four chapters containing policy discourse are Chapter 7 (The Road to Redistributing Wealth), Chapter 8 (Taxing Multinationals or Taxing Wealthy Individuals?), Chapter 9 (Global versus Unilateral Perspectives on Tax Justice), and Chapter 10 (Emancipation, Redistribution and Sustainability). Clearly, the policies are all in respect of moderating and modulating income and wealth inequalities. An additional inequality dimension covered is the "inequalities in carbon emissions".

From Five Books[9] on Inequality[10]

Since the turn of the century, dozens of books have been published on income and wealth inequality – global as well as country specific. Of these, the relatively more popular and influential were the books by the 2001 economics Nobel prize winner Joseph Stiglitz, Thomas Piketty, and Branko Milanovic. The books' policy discourse is summarized next.

Stiglitz (2012/13): The Price of Inequality

The book is predominantly about the relatively more recent increases in income and wealth inequality in the United States. A key point is that while market forces create inequality, government policies should work to moderate it. Why? Because relatively high inequality can lead to economic and social instability.

Stiglitz (2015): The Great Divide

This is a collection of articles: 49 articles in all with a high 33 from the *New York Times* (16) and *Project Syndicate* (17). The great income divide in America and its many causes and consequences are a core subject of the volume.

Piketty (2014): Capital in the Twenty-First Century

Like Stiglitz, Piketty too showcases the "high" level of inequality across parts of the industrialized world, with the United States in the "top" spot. It is noted that returns to capital exceed GDP growth rate, and the trend may continue, leading to extreme wealth concentration. In his review of the Piketty book, Martin Wolf (*Financial Times*, August 15, 2014) says that the recommendations such as "far higher marginal tax rates on top incomes and a progressive global wealth tax" are bold and "unrealistic".

Piketty (2015): The Economics of Inequality

In the "note to the reader" upfront, the author points out that the book is an update of his 1997 work. Much to the possible surprise of Piketty, Paul Krugman, in his review of the book (*New York Times*, August 2, 2015) says: "Let me be blunt: I don't know how the decision was made to release this". And also: "readers who see only this volume will end up placing far too much faith in a story that emphasizes the invisible hand of the market, and too little on the visible role of powerful institutions".

Milanovic (2016): Global Inequality – A New Approach for the Age of Globalization

The last chapter has *ten short reflections on the future of income inequality and globalization*. One of the reflections concluded that in the future, wage inequality will tend to rise. The tenth and final reflection is just one simple question: will inequality disappear as globalization continues? The answer too is straight and simple: "No. The gains from globalization will not be evenly distributed".

The Consensus

The good news is the consensus among economists about the need to address the issue of inequality (see box, given next).

"Economists now embrace the role of fiscal policy in a way not obvious in previous surveys and are largely supportive of government policies that mitigate income inequality". This was the finding of Doris Geide-Stevenson and Alvaro La Parra Perez in their December 2021 paper comprising the survey of opinions of members of the American Economic Association. The percentage of respondents who felt that the distribution of income in America should be more equal rose from 68% in 2000 to 86% in 2020–2021. (*Consensus among economists 2020 – A sharpening of the picture*, Weber State University, December 2021.)

Annex 5

Adequate Housing is a Human Right

Introduction

The Universal Declaration of Human Rights was adopted by the United Nations General Assembly on December 10, 1948, just months after the formal ending of the Second World War. The matter for this entire annex is sourced from the most comprehensive website *www.ohchr.org/en* (accessed July 11–12, 2023). OHCHR refers to the *Office of the High Commissioner for Human Rights*, the leading human rights entity of the United Nations.

Notes from OHCHR on Housing

The page with info on housing (*www.ohchr.org/en/topic/land-and-housing*) has four topic links, including: the right to adequate housing and Special Rapporteur on adequate housing. About housing, here is an excerpt from the site:

[I]nternational human rights law does recognize everyone's right to . . . adequate housing. Still, over a billion people live in substandard housing, slums and informal settlements. . . . Millions are subject to forced eviction or other conditions which impede the right to live in security, peace and dignity.

About Special Rapporteur (SR)

[O]n 17 April 2000, the Commission on Human Rights adopted resolution 2000/9 in which it decided to establish, . . . a Special Rapporteur whose mandate would focus on adequate housing as a component of the right to an adequate standard of living.

"Since the mandate of the Special Rapporteur on the right to adequate housing was established, the respective mandate holders undertook numerous country visits and submitted various thematic reports". (In April 2020, Prof Balakrishnan Rajagopal[11] took charge as Special Rapporteur.)

Inputs Sought by SR

In connection with submitting his report to the 78th session of the General Assembly of the United Nations to be presented in October 2023, the SR sought inputs from different countries and institutions on the right to adequate housing. The report "*A place to live in dignity for all, make housing affordable*" will be based on the responses to a comprehensive and well-drafted questionnaire. The questionnaire covers the following topics: National law, policies and jurisprudence relating to affordable housing; data and trends on housing affordability; causes and consequences of housing unaffordability; *and* laws, policies, programmes, and practices aiming to ensure that housing is affordable to all without discrimination.

From out of several submissions from different countries and institutions, those from India and Indonesia are summarized in the next section. Two submissions were received from India: from the Centre for Sustainable Development, Law and Policy, REVA University; and the Centre for the Sustainable use of Natural and Social Resources (CSNR), based in Odisha. One submission was from the Government of Indonesia.

Salient Points from an Indian Submission

Three faculty members of the Centre for Sustainable Development, Law, and Policy; School of Legal Studies, REVA University made a comprehensive submission. Given next is a short summary of selected topics/submissions.

National law, policies, and jurisprudence relating to affordable housing

India has various laws and constitutional provisions that aim to ensure affordable housing and provide guarantees for a minimum standard of living. The Supreme Court has held that "right to shelter is a fundamental right, which springs from the right to residence guaranteed under Article 19(1)(e) and the right to life guaranteed under Article 21".

Housing Policies and Schemes

The National Urban Housing and Habitat Policy 2007 aims to provide affordable housing to urban poor households. The Pradhan Mantri Awas Yojana launched in 2015 aims at providing affordable housing to all eligible beneficiaries by 2022.

Important Supreme Court decisions on the issue of affordable housing

- In a 1985 judgment, SC held that the government has an obligation to provide housing to the homeless and the poor. Evicting them without providing alternative housing is unconstitutional.
- In a 2000 judgement, SC directed the central and state governments to take steps to provide housing to the urban poor and slum dwellers.

Causes and Consequences of Housing Unaffordability

- As per a study conducted by the Ministry of Housing and Urban Poverty Alleviation, the urban housing shortage in India is currently estimated at about 19 million. This gap is expected to further widen to an estimated 38 million homes by 2030 largely due to the rising population and increased urbanization via rural to urban migration.
- Without Government support, the limited availability of land in urban areas makes it unviable for developers to take up housing projects. Further, the substantial non-marketable urban lands used by Government-owned entities such as railways can be used more efficiently.
- Developers often face several hurdles on the regulatory approvals front. In addition, they need to coordinate with multiple government and municipal departments which translates to a substantial delay in commencing construction of a project. These cause cost escalations.

The Eviction Problem

- (There is no official data on evictions.) Housing rights campaigners warned in recent times that more than 250,000 people were evicted across India during the COVID pandemic.

- From March 2020 through July 2021, authorities demolished more than 43,000 homes and evicted about 21 people every hour, according to the Housing and Land Rights Network (HLRN), an advocacy group in Delhi. In nearly all cases, officials did not follow due process including giving sufficient notice, and a majority of those evicted did not receive compensation from the government, HLRN said in its annual report.
- Nearly 16 million people are at risk of being evicted and displaced, according to HLRN, including about 2 million whose claims to forest land have been rejected. Last year alone, more than 170,000 people were removed from their homes, it said, compared to about 107,000 people the previous year. Court orders make it easier to carry out evictions, and slum dwellers often have no legal recourse.

Some of the Relevant Acts

- The Right to Fair Compensation and Transparency in Land Acquisition, Rehabilitation and Resettlement Act that came into force on January 1, 2014.
- The Protection of Human Rights Act, 1993.
- The Slum Areas (Improvement and Clearance) Act, 1956.
- The Street Vendors (Protection of Livelihood and Regulation of Street Vending) Act 2014.

Relevant National Policies

- The stated focus of India's National Urban Housing and Habitat Policy 2007 is the "Provision of 'Affordable Housing for All' with special emphasis on vulnerable sections of society such as Scheduled Castes/Scheduled Tribes, Backward Classes, Minorities and the urban poor".
- Announced in 2009, the Rajiv Awas Yojana (RAY) is a national scheme of the Ministry of Housing and Urban Poverty Alleviation that intends to, "build a 'slum free' country while providing shelter and basic services to the urban poor".

Assessment of Some of the Schemes/Policies

Pradhan Mantri Awas Yojana (PMAY) with its credit-linked subsidy scheme (CLSS) was introduced to provide its beneficiaries an interest subsidy to avail loans to purchase or build a house. This scheme is primarily targeted towards the EWS and LIG segment. As per latest data available in the PMAY records, about 12.3 million houses have been sanctioned under the scheme, of which about 6.3 million houses have been completed with total investment of INR 8.3 lakh crores.

Salient Points from the Indonesian Submission

The following is a short summary of the submission by the Government of Indonesia.

National law, policies, and jurisprudence relating to affordable housing

Indonesia's 1945 Constitution states: "Every person has the right to a prosperous life, both physically and mentally, a place to live, and a good and healthy environment, and has the right to obtain health services". Furthermore, Article 40 of Law No. 39 of 1999 on Human Rights states that every person has the right to a decent place to live and a decent standard of living.

Housing affordability increase/decreased over the past ten years

The percentage of households at the bottom 40% of income distribution, which occupy liveable houses increased every year from 2015 to 2022. This indicates that the number of households with vulnerable financial capabilities who can access adequate housing improved every year.

Households, persons, or groups at particular risk of being exposed to housing affordability

Informal workers account for a dominant share (60%) of the Indonesian workforce, comprising 77 million individuals or 31 million households, of which there are over 4 million housing ownership backlogs and over 7 million uninhabitable houses.

Policies or laws which seek to control the price of land

A special agency called the Land Bank Agency is established with special authority to manage state land. The Land Bank serves to control the value/price of land and prevents land speculation. Currently, the Ministry of Agrarian and Spatial Planning/National Land Agency is in the process of establishing a national land pricing system to achieve equitable land values.

Policies, programmes and practices aiming to ensure that housing is affordable to all

- The national policy direction and strategy for the housing sector are laid out in the National Medium-Term Development Plan 2020–2024. It aims at increasing people's access to decent, safe, and affordable housing to achieve an inclusive and liveable city.

- Housing development policy is also directed at improving people's access to decent housing through collaborative programmes, such as community-based housing provision in various districts.
- Self-build Housing Stimulus Assistance: the government provides financial assistance to low-income families to improve the quality of their houses as well as its infrastructure, facilities, and general utilities. In addition, to increase community self-reliance in building liveable homes independently, the Directorate General of Housing has the Self-build Housing Clinic programme, which facilitates self-build housing provision and provides guidance to individuals in building or repairing self-build housing.
- National Affordable Housing Program (NAHP): The program's goal is one of helping individuals and families in poverty to be able to own a residence and increase the quality of housing which they own through the development of housing finance schemes, strengthening the implementation system of the self-build housing program, and encouraging reforms in the development of decent and affordable housing programs and policies in Indonesia. This program was developed through the cooperation between the Government of Indonesia's Ministry of Public Work and Housing and the World Bank.

Annex 6

The UN System[12]

This Annex is a short note listing the various United Nations organizations (including specialized agencies), their essential objectives, and roles.

Organization and Headquarters	*Key objectives/roles*
1. UN Development Programme (UNDP), *New York City, United States*	Works in nearly 170 countries and territories, helping to eradicate poverty, reduce inequalities, and build resilience so that countries can sustain progress.
2. UN Environment Programme (UNEP), *Nairobi, Kenya*	Promotes the wise use and sustainable development of the global environment.
3. UN Population Fund (UNFPA), *New York City, United States*	Agency for delivering a world where every pregnancy is wanted and every birth is safe.
4. UN Human Settlements Programme (UN-HABITAT), *Nairobi, Kenya*	Promoting socially and environmentally sustainable human settlements' development and the *achievement of adequate shelter for all.*
5. UN Children's Fund (UNICEF), *New York City, United States*	Works in 190 countries and territories to save children's lives, to defend their rights, and to help them fulfil their potential, from early childhood through adolescence.

(*Continued*)

(Continued)

Organization and Headquarters	*Key objectives/roles*
6. World Food Programme (WFP), *Rome, Italy*	Aims to eradicate hunger and malnutrition. Helps almost 100 million people in about 88 countries with assistance every year through food or cash distributions and more.
7. Food and Agriculture Organization (FAO), *Rome, Italy*	Leads international efforts to fight hunger. A forum for negotiating agreements between developing and developed countries and a source of knowledge and information to aid development.
8. International Civil Aviation Organization (ICAO), *Montreal, Canada*	Develops standards for global air transport and assists its 192 Member States in sharing the world's skies for their socio-economic benefit.
9. International Fund for Agricultural Development (IFAD), *Rome, Italy*	Works with poor rural populations in developing countries to eliminate poverty, hunger, and malnutrition; raise their productivity and incomes; and improve the quality of their lives.
10. International Labor Organization (ILO), *Geneva, Switzerland*	Promotes international labour rights by formulating international standards relating to worker rights.
11. International Monetary Fund (IMF), *Washington, DC, United States*	Provides temporary financial assistance to countries to help ease balance of payments' adjustment and technical assistance.
12. International Maritime Organization (IMO), *London, United Kingdom*	Created a comprehensive shipping regulatory framework
13. International Telecommunication Union (ITU), *Geneva, Switzerland*	Committed to connecting all the people of the world
14. United Nations Educational, Scientific and Cultural Organization, (UNESCO), *Paris, France*	Focuses on everything from teacher training to helping improve education worldwide to protecting important historical and cultural sites around the world.
15. United Nations Industrial Development Organization (UNIDO), *Vienna, Austria*	Promotes industrial development for poverty reduction, inclusive globalization, and environmental sustainability.
16. World Tourism Organization (UNWTO), *Madrid, Spain*	Promotes responsible, sustainable, and universally accessible tourism
17. Universal Postal Union (UPU), *Bern, Switzerland*	Forum for cooperation between postal sector players.
18. World Health Organization, (WHO) *Geneva, Switzerland*	As the directing and coordinating authority on international health, the objective of WHO is the attainment of the highest possible level of health by all peoples.
19. World Intellectual Property Organization (WIPO), *Geneva, Switzerland*	Protects intellectual property throughout the world through 23 international treaties.

Organization and Headquarters	*Key objectives/roles*
20. World Meteorological Organization (WMO), *Geneva, Switzerland*	Facilitates the free international exchange of meteorological data and information and the furtherance of its use in aviation, shipping, security, and agriculture.
21. World Bank Group, *Washington, DC, USA*	Focuses on poverty reduction and the improvement of living standards by providing low-interest loans, interest-free credit, and grants to developing countries.
22. UN Programme on HIV/ AIDS (UNAIDS), *Geneva, Switzerland*	Leads and inspires the world to achieve its shared vision of zero new HIV infections, zero discrimination, and zero AIDS-related deaths.
23 UN High Commissioner for Refugees (UNHCR), *Geneva, Switzerland*	Protects refugees worldwide and facilitates their return home or resettlement.
24. UN Institute for Disarmament Research (UNIDIR), *Geneva, Switzerland*	Generates ideas and promotes action on disarmament and security.
25. UN Institute for Training and Research (UNITAR), *Geneva, Switzerland*	Training arm of the United Nations System
26. UN Office for Project Services (UNOPS), *Copenhagen, Denmark*	Helps the UN, governments, and other partners to manage projects and procurement in an efficient way.
27. UN Relief and Works Agency (UNRWA), *Amman, Jordan*	Contributes to the welfare and human development of the four generations of Palestine refugees.
28. UN System Staff College (UNSSC), *Turin, Italy*	Designs and delivers learning programmes for the staff of the UN system and its partners.
29. UN University (UNU), *Tokyo, Japan*	Comprises 14 research and training institutes in 12 countries. As the think tank of the UN system, it provides policymakers with high-quality, evidence-based research and pragmatic advice.
30. UN Women, *New York City, USA*	Focuses on gender equality and women's empowerment.
31. Preparatory Commission for the Comprehensive Nuclear-Test-Ban Treaty Organization (CTBTO), *Vienna, Austria*	Promotes the Comprehensive Nuclear-Test-Ban Treaty (which is not yet in force) and the build-up of the verification regime so that it is operational when the Treaty enters into force.
32. International Atomic Energy Agency (IAEA), *Vienna, Austria*	Works to promote the safe, secure, and peaceful use of nuclear technologies.
33. International Criminal Court (ICC), *The Hague, Netherlands*	Investigates and, where warranted, tries individuals charged with the gravest crimes of concern to the international community: genocide, war crimes, crimes against humanity, and the crime of aggression. As a court of last resort, it seeks to complement, not replace, national courts.

(Continued)

(Continued)

Organization and Headquarters	Key objectives/roles
34. International Organization for Migration (IOM), *Geneva, Switzerland*	Works to help ensure the orderly and humane management of migration and promotes international cooperation on migration issues.
35. Organization for the Prohibition of Chemical Weapons (OPCW), *The Hague, Netherlands*	Implementing body of the Chemical Weapons Convention (CWC), which entered into force in 1997.
36. United Nations Framework Convention on Climate Change (UNFCCC), *Bonn, Germany*	Tasked with supporting the global response to the threat of climate change.
37. World Trade Organization (WTO), *Geneva, Switzerland*	Forum for governments to negotiate trade agreements and a place where member governments try to sort out the trade problems they face with each other.
38. International Trade Centre (ITC), *Geneva, Switzerland*	The only development agency that is fully dedicated to supporting the internationalization of small- and medium-sized enterprises (SMEs).

The 38 UN Agencies by Headquarters Location[13]

HQ Location (No. of agencies)	Organizations
New York City, United States (4)	UNDP, UNFPA, UNICEF, UN-Women
Washington, DC, United States (2)	IMF, World Bank
Nairobi, Kenya (2)	UNEP, UN-HABITAT
Rome, Italy (3)	WFP, FAO, IFAD
Turin, Italy (1)	UN System Staff College
Montreal, Canada (1)	ICAO
Geneva, Switzerland (12)	ILO, ITU, WHO, WIPO, WMO, WTO, ITC, UNAIDS, UNHCR, UNIDIR, UNITAR, IOM
Bern, Switzerland (1)	Universal Postal Union
London, United Kingdom (1)	International Maritime Organization
Paris, France (1)	UNESCO
Vienna, Austria (3)	UNIDO, CTBTO, IAEA
Madrid, Spain (1)	World Tourism Organization
Copenhagen, Denmark (1)	UNOPS
Amman, Jordan (1)	UN Relief and Works Agency (UNRWA)
Tokyo, Japan (1)	UNU
The Hague, Netherlands (2)	International Criminal Court (ICC) Organization for the Prohibition of Chemical Weapons (OPCW)
Bonn, Germany (1)	United Nations Framework Convention on Climate Change (UNFCCC)

In Sum

Geneva, Switzerland 12; New York City, United States 4; Rome, Italy 3; Vienna, Austria 3; Washington, DC, United States 2; *Nairobi, Kenya 2*; The Hague, Netherlands 2
One agency each located at
Turin (Italy), Montreal (Canada), Bern (Switzerland), London (UK), Paris (France), Madrid (Spain), Copenhagen (Denmark), *Amman (Jordan)*, Tokyo (Japan), *and* Bonn (Germany) [In total 10].

Annex 7

Future of the UN System: Possibilities for Consideration

Organization and Role	*Possible Action*
UNDP: Helping to eradicate poverty, reduce inequalities, and help countries to sustain progress.	Merger with World Bank Group
UNEP: Preserving the global environment	The one and only new organization to oversee all issues pertaining to climate change and the environment
UNFPA: Safe and desired child births	To be a part of WHO
UN-HABITAT: Environmentally sustainable human settlements' development and the achievement of adequate shelter for all.	Strengthening the organization to take up on-ground action (Chapter 6 has a bit more detail).
UNICEF: Saving children's lives and help them fulfil their potential, from early childhood through adolescence.	To be part of WHO and UNESCO
WFP: Assistance every year through food or cash distributions and more.	Transfer the activity to national governments.
FAO: Leads international efforts to fight hunger.	To be the single agency for food security across the globe.
ICAO: Assists its 192 Member States in sharing the world's skies	Continues as it is.
IFAD: Eliminates poverty, hunger, and malnutrition across poor rural populations	To be integrated with FAO
ILO: Promotes international labour rights	Continues as it is.
IMF and World Bank	Experts to explore the future changes.
IMO: Created a comprehensive shipping regulatory framework	Continues as it is.
ITU: Committed to connecting all the world's people	Continues as it is.
UNESCO: Focuses on everything from teacher training to helping improve education worldwide, etc.	To be strengthened to become the single key agency to promote common education standards across the globe.
UNIDO: Promotes industrial development	To be integrated with the World Bank

(*Continued*)

(Continued)

Organization and Role	Possible Action
World Tourism Organization	No specific need for such an organization – activity belongs to national governments
Universal Postal Union	Continues as it is
WHO: Coordinating authority on international health	To be the one and only organization to ensure national and local health care activities.
WIPO: Protects intellectual property throughout the world	Continues as it is.
WMO: Facilitates the free exchange of meteorological data	Continues as it is.
UNAIDS: Vision of zero new HIV infections, zero discrimination, and zero AIDS-related deaths.	To be integrated with WHO
UNHCR: Protecting refugees and facilitating their return home or resettlement.	Should work out globally agreed refugee rules and then close operations.
UNIDIR: Generates ideas and promotes action on disarmament and security.	Should work out the future action agenda for total disarmament and then close operations.
UNITAR: Training arm of the United Nations System	Why not make use of globally well ranked public policy institutions?
UNOPS: Helps in managing projects and procurements.	National governments and UN system organizations to take on the work.
UNRWA: Contributed to the welfare of four generations of Palestine refugees.	No end in sight? Delegate operations to voluntary organizations and close the agency.
UN System Staff College	Why not make use of globally well ranked public policy institutions?
UN University	Best option is to award research grants from a UN Research Fund
UN Women: Works for gender equality and women empowerment.	To evolve into an excellent institution with expansion globally
CTBTO: Promotes the Comprehensive Nuclear-Test-Ban Treaty (not yet in force)	Should work on a time plan and redefine its role
IAEA: Promoting safe, secure, and peaceful use of nuclear technologies.	May consider changing the aim to setting up rules and be the monitoring agency.
International Criminal Court	Continues as it is.
International Organization for Migration	To work out global rules and be the monitoring agency
Organization for the Prohibition of Chemical Weapons	Time-bound actions and planned closure may be feasible.
UNFCCC: Supporting the global response to the threat of climate change.	To evolve into an organization for promoting minimal climate change with national agencies support.
WTO: Forum for trade agreements and negotiations.	Continues as it is.
ITC: For supporting the internationalization of SMEs	Promote relevant national actions and then end operations

Notes

1 SDGs succeed the earlier Millennium Development Goals ending in 2015.
2 United Nations (2023), *Progress Towards the Sustainable Development Goals: Towards a Rescue Plan for People and Planet, Report of the Secretary-General (Special Edition)*, Advance Unedited Version, United Nations, May.
3 Arrow, Kenneth J., Bernheim, B. Douglas, Feldstein, Martins, McFadden, Daniell, Poterba, James M. and Solow, Robert M. (2011), "100 Years of the American Economic Review: The Top 20 Articles", *The American Economic Review*, 101, 1–8, February.
4 Alfani, Guido (2021), "Economic Inequality in Preindustrial Times: Europe and Beyond", *Journal of Economic Literature*, 59(1), 3–44.
5 From World Wealth Distribution and Income Inequality 2022 by Lucas Ventura, www.gfmag.com/global-data/economic-data/wealth-distribution-income-inequality (Accessed January 15, 2022).
6 An academic friend of the authors, hailing from Germany, once commented about the high marginal income tax in his country as follows: "Yes, we pay high taxes. But then our health care is taken care of even after our retirement and through the ageing process".
7 The Gini ratio/index/coefficient developed by Corrado Gini in 1912 has since been widely used to measure the extent of inequality in income/wealth. The index ranges from 0 to 1, depicting respectively no inequality whatsoever and the highest inequality (just one enjoying all while no one else has even a dime).
8 Data are from https://worldpopulationreview.com/country-rankings/income-inequality-by-country (Accessed February 23, 2022). This source cites the *World Economic Forum Inclusive Development Index*.
9 Stiglitz, Joseph (2012, 2013), *The Price of Inequality*, W.W. Norton and Penguin Books; Stiglitz, Joseph (2015), *The Great Divide*, Allen Lane; Piketty, Thomas (2014), *Capital in the Twenty-First Century*, Harvard University Press; Piketty, Thomas (2015), *The Economics of Inequality*, Belknap Press of the Harvard University Press; Milanovic, Branko (2016), *Global Inequality: A New Approach for the Age of Globalization*, Belknap Press of the Harvard University Press.
10 This entire section is a crisp summary of a very detailed appendix in *Human Evolution, Economic Progress and Evolutionary Failure*, by the author (Routledge, 2017, 2019, and 2021).
11 Professor of Law and Development at the Department of Urban Studies and Planning at the Massachusetts Institute of Technology.
12 www.un.org/en/about-us/un-system (Accessed April 20, 2023).
13 Based on the information at www.un.org/en/about-us/un-system (Accessed April 20, 2023).

Statistical Annex

(Covering 17 countries making up two-thirds of the world population)

Data source is the World Bank's World Development Indicators, except when stated otherwise.

Table 1 Water, sanitation, and health indicators, 2022

Country	Undernourished (% of population)	Access to improved sanitation (proportion of population)	Access to improved water source (proportion of population)	Satisfaction with water quality (proportion of population)	Satisfaction with the availability of quality healthcare (proportion of population)
Bangladesh	9.7	0.7639	0.9929	0.81	0.725
Brazil	2.5	0.8932	0.9991	0.725	0.38
China	2.5	0.7638	0.9992	0.78	0.75
Congo, DR	41.7	0.4866	0.5526	0.38	0.39
Egypt	5.4	0.9992	0.9933	0.625	0.395
Ethiopia	16.2	0.1246	0.5749	0.545	0.495
India	15.3	0.7161	0.9245	0.825	0.76
Indonesia	6.5	0.8687	0.6632	0.88	0.76
Iran	5.5	0.9992	0.9992	0.615	0.48
Japan	2.5	0.9862	0.9991	0.875	0.735
Mexico	7.2	0.9588	0.9844	0.73	0.475
Nigeria	14.6	0.6937	0.6652	0.675	0.465
Pakistan	12.9	0.7363	0.9672	0.595	0.465
The Philippines	9.4	0.9125	0.9077	0.82	0.805
Russia	2.5	0.9769	0.9991	0.615	0.365
The United States	2.5	0.9563	0.999	0.855	0.805
Vietnam	6.7	0.8199	0.9537	0.8	0.74

Table 2 Out-of-pocket expense and data on physicians and nurses

	Out-of-pocket % of current, 2020	Physicians per 1,000 people, 2014–2019	Nurses and midwives per 1,000 people, 2014–2019
Bangladesh	74.0	0.6	0.4
Brazil	22.4	2.3	7.4
China	34.8	2.2	3.1
Congo, DR	39.7	0.4	1.1
Egypt	59.3	0.7	1.9
Ethiopia	33.1	0.1	0.7
India	50.6	0.7	1.7
Indonesia	31.8	0.5	3.8
Iran	37.1	1.6	2.1
Japan	12.6	2.5	11.9
Mexico	38.8	2.4	2.8
Nigeria	74.7	0.4	1.5
Pakistan	55.4	1.1	0.5
The Philippines	45.0	0.6	5.4
Russia	27.8	4.2	8.5
The United States	9.9	2.6	15.7
Vietnam	39.6	0.8	1.4

Table 3 Incidence of tuberculosis and diabetes, 2021

Country	Tuberculosis per 100,000 people	Diabetes % of those in 20–79 years of age
Bangladesh	221	14
Brazil	48	9
China	55	11
Congo, DR	318	6
Egypt	10	21
Ethiopia	119	5
India	210	10
Indonesia	354	11
Iran	12	9
Japan	11	7
Mexico	25	17
Nigeria	219	4
Pakistan	264	31
The Philippines	650	7
Russia	47	6
The United States	3	11
Vietnam	173	6

Table 4 Health system ranks

Country	Health care system rank	LPI 2020 rank
Japan	**2**	19
The United States	30	**18**
Russia	46	76
China	51	54
Brazil	65	70
Mexico	77	68
Vietnam	87	73
Indonesia	88	57
The Philippines	89	83
Iran	94	120
India	117	101
Egypt	130	121
Bangladesh	131	125
Congo, DR	142	**161**
Ethiopia	150	150
Pakistan	151	138
Nigeria	**153**	144

Source: https://worldpopulationreview.com/country-rankings/best-healthcare-in-the-world (Accessed July 18, 2023).

Note: Lowest and highest ranks are indicated in bold

Table 5 Countries with highest to lowest health expenditure percentage of GDP

Country name	2000–2009	2010–2019	2020
The United States	14.4	16.4	18.8
Japan	7.7	10.5	10.9
Brazil	8.3	8.6	10.3
Russia	5.1	5.2	7.6
Mexico	5.5	5.6	6.2
China	4.2	4.8	5.6
Iran	5.1	6.7	5.3
The Philippines	3.4	4	5.1
Vietnam	4	4.8	4.7
Egypt	4.9	4.9	4.4
Congo, DR	3.8	3.7	4.1
Ethiopia	4.6	4	3.5
Indonesia	2.3	2.9	3.4
Nigeria	3.8	3.4	3.4
India	3.8	3.3	3
Pakistan	2.6	2.5	2.9
Bangladesh	2.4	2.7	2.6

Table 6 Top 64 countries on life expectancy (LE) and rank (R)

Country	LE	R	Country	LE	R	Country	LE	R
Hong Kong	85	1	Ireland	82	22	Kuwait	79	43
Macao	85	2	New Zealand	82	23	New Caledonia	79	44
Japan	84	3	Austria	81	24	Qatar	79	45
Korea, Rep.	84	4	Channel Islands	81	25	Thailand	79	46
Liechtenstein	84	5	Cyprus	81	26	The UAE	79	47
Switzerland	84	6	Denmark	81	27	Antigua and Barbuda	78	48
Australia	83	7	Germany	81	28	Barbados	78	49
Canada	83	8	Isle of Man	81	29	China	78	50
Faroe Islands	83	9	The Netherlands	81	30	Costa Rica	77	51
Iceland	83	10	Portugal	81	31	Czechia	77	52
Israel	83	11	Slovenia	81	32	Estonia	77	53
Italy	83	12	The United Kingdom	81	33	Guam	77	54
Luxembourg	83	13	Greece	80	34	Kosovo	77	55
Malta	83	14	Maldives	80	35	Saudi Arabia	77	56
Norway	83	15	Puerto Rico	80	36	Albania	76	57
Singapore	83	16	St. Martin (France)	80	37	Algeria	76	58
Spain	83	17	Virgin Islands (the United States)	80	38	Croatia	76	59
Sweden	83	18	Bahrain	79	39	Panama	76	60
Belgium	82	19	Bermuda	79	40	Poland	76	61
Finland	82	20	Chile	79	41	Sri Lanka	76	62
France	82	21	French Polynesia	79	42	Türkiye	76	63
						The United States	**76**	**64**

Note: Bold values represent the US lagging behind

Table 7 Educational access equality and percentage with no schooling, 2022

Country	Equal access to quality education (0 unequal, 4 equal)	% of population with no schooling
Bangladesh	0.6	30.4
Brazil	0.7	8.8
China	1.6	6.9
Congo, DR	1.3	15.4
Egypt	0.4	19.2
Ethiopia	1.6	5.3
India	0.9	29.8
Indonesia	1.0	7.2
Iran	2.4	24.1
Japan	3.9	0.1
Mexico	1.0	7.5
Nigeria	0.7	32.6
Pakistan	0.2	39.3
The Philippines	0.9	3.2
Russia	2.4	0.2
The United States	2.4	0.6
Vietnam	2.6	4.3

Source: Social Progress Index (see Annex 1.3 for more details).

Table 8 World Economic Forum's Global Gender Gap Index: components and weights

Category-wise sub-indexes	Weights
Economic Participation and Opportunity	
Labour-force participation rate, % (females-to-males, ratio)	0.199
Wage equality for similar work (survey) (females-to-males, ratio)	0.310
Estimated earned income, PPP, int. $ (females-to-males, ratio)	0.221
Legislators, senior officials and managers, % (females-to-males, ratio)	0.149
Professional and technical workers, % (females-to-males, ratio)	0.121
Educational Attainment	
Literacy rate, % (females-to-males, ratio)	0.191
Enrolment in primary education, % (females-to-males, ratio)	0.459
Enrolment in secondary education, % (females-to-males, ratio)	0.230
Enrolment in tertiary education, % (females-to-males, ratio)	0.121
Health and Survival	
Sex ratio at birth, % (females-to-males, ratio)	0.693
Healthy life expectancy, years (females-to-males, ratio)	0.307
Political Empowerment	
Women in parliament, % (females-to-males, ratio)	0.310
Women in ministerial positions, % (females-to-males, ratio)	0.247
Years with female head of state (last 50), share of tenure years (females-to-males, ratio)	0.443

Source: World Economic Forum, *Global Gender Gap Report 2023*, p. 65.

Note: GGGI is the simple average of the four components

Table 9 Net Food Trade and Food Security Index

Country	Population 2021 (million)	Net Food Trade 2020 ($ million)	Per capita net trade ($)	Global Food Security Index	GFSI Rank within 17
Bangladesh	169	−7,959	−47	54	11
Brazil	214	63,279	296	65.1	6
China	1412	−1,13,955	−81	74.2	3
Congo, DR	96	−595	−6	43	14
Egypt	109	−8469	−8	56	10
Ethiopia	120	27	0	44.5	13
India	1407	13,450	10	58.9	9
Indonesia	273	19,038	70	60.2	7
Iran	88	−3905	−44	NA	NA
Japan	125	−49,998	−400	79.5	1
Mexico	126	15,311	122	69.1	4
Nigeria	213	−5,785	−27	42	15
Pakistan	231	−2,723	−12	52.2	12
The Philippines	113	−4,841	−43	59.3	8
Russian Fed.	143	731	5	69.1	4
The United States	331	−26,351	−80	78	2
Vietnam	97	8,316	86	67.9	5

Sources of basic data: FAO Statistical Yearbook 2022 for the first two columns and *The Global Food Security Index 2022*, developed by Economist Impact and supported by Corteva Agriscience, for the last two columns.

Index

Note: Page locators in **bold** indicate a table on the corresponding page.

accountability 18, 22
affordable housing 10, 71–75
Afghanistan 43
AIDS/HIV 25, 60, 77
Alfani, Guido 2, 6, 65, 66, 81

Baker, Emma 8, 14,
Beijing, China 10–11, 15, 21
Bentley, Rebecca 8, 14,
Bess, Michael D. 52, 53
Bharatiya Janata Party, India 45
Bhaumik, Mani 1, 6
Blanchard, Oliver 3, 6

Cambridge International Examinations
	(CIE) 37
capital cities 7–9
capitalism 14, 57, 68
Central Board of Secondary Education
	(CBSE) 37
Centre for Global Development 38
Centre for the Sustainable use of Natural
	and Social Resources (CSNR) 71
child health 25, 26
China: compulsory education 32–33;
	economy 10–11; educational
	proficiency 29, **30**, 31; food
	security 50; health insurance
	system 20–21; health
	expenditure 20–21; population
	11; private education 32, **36**;
	school 32–34; secondary
	education 33; slum/homeless
	population **8**; pupil-teacher ratio
	30, **31**; vocational education 34
Climate Challenge 53

climate change 4, 48, 52, 54, 78–80
Commonwealth Fund 23–24, 27
Commonwealth Fund Commission 23, 27
communicable diseases 19, 25, 26, 63;
	see also disease
Communist Party 10, 32
Comprehensive Nuclear-Test-Ban Treaty
	Organization (CTBTO) 77–78, 80
Council for the Indian School Certificate
	Examination (CISCE) 37
COVID-19 2, 8, 23, 25, 27, 35, 39, 72
creation 1, 40
credit-linked subsidy scheme (CLSS) 73
cross-country trends 5, 16, 28
CTBTO *see* Comprehensive Nuclear-
	Test-Ban Treaty Organization

debt relief 19
Delhi Urban Shelter Improvement Board
	(DUSIB) 12
diabetes 16, **17**, **83**, 88
disadvantaged 4, 33
disarmament 49, 77, 80
discrimination 4, 8, 61, 63, 64, 71, 77, 80
disease 2, 16, 19, 25, 26, 27, 63

education: access to 62–63; advanced
	28–29, **30**, 43–44, 63;
	educational aid 2, 37–38; exams
	33, 37; higher 28, 34, 38, 43, 44,
	53; inclusive 35, 36, 38; literacy
	43, 60, **86**; moral 33; quality 3,
	29, 32, 33, 36, 38, 52, 59–60,
	62–63, **85**; standardization 37;
	vocational 33, 34
employment 47, 60, 63, 65

empowerment. *see* women empowerment
equality is human 1; *see also* visible
    equality
Ethnic Integration Policy 13, 14
ethnicity 13–14, 61–62, 67
expenditure 3, 20, 22–23, 53, *84*
experts 24, 53, 79

FAO *see* Food and Agriculture
    Organization
Food and Agriculture Organization
    (FAO) 48, 51, 76, 78–78
food security 50–51, 53, 79
food trade 50, 86
France: educational aid 38, 76; life
    expectancy *85*

GDP *see* gross domestic product
gender bias 41, 46, 57
gender equality 3, 28, 38, 40–41, 45, 46,
    47, 52, 59, 60, 61, 62, 77, 80
gender inequality 40–41, 43
Gender Inequality Index (GII) 41, **42**,
    42–43, 47
General Certificate of Education (GCE) 37
Germany 38, 64, 67, 78, 81, **85**
GGGI *see* Global Gender Gap Index
GII *see* Gender Inequality Index
Gini: income 10, 67, 68; ratio 40, 67–68;
    wealth 67, 68
Gini, Corrado 40
global: education system 37; food
    security 51; gender gap 42, **86**;
    population 5
Global Food Security Index (GFSI) 50,
    53, 86
Global Gender Gap Index (GGGI) 42, **86**
Global Grade Twelve (GGT) 37–38
global warming 53
globalization 14, 37, 69–70, 76
green economy 4
greenhouse gas 53
gross domestic product 3, 23
Grusky, David 2, 6

habitat 7, 14, 54, 72
Harvard Business School 3
health insurance 20, 21, 22
healthcare: overall access to **13**, 16, **17**,
    18–19, 25, 63; right to health
    18; system 22–23
Hill, Jasmine 2
homeless 7, **8**, 9, 12, 15, 72

housing: health connection **14**; inequality
    8–10, 14, 52; property 10;
    subsidy 8, 73
Housing and Land Rights Network
    (HLRN) 73
Housing Development Board, Singapore
    (HDB) 13
Human Development Report 1990 3

IFAD *see* International Fund for
    Agricultural Development
IMF *see* International Monetary Fund
inclusive/inclusiveness 7, 9, 46, 63, 74
income: Gini 10, 67–68; inequality 2,
    65–66, 68–70 (*see also* wealth
    inequality); median 67–38;
    national 8, 60
India: education equality 28, **29–31**, 35–37;
    food security **50**; gender equality
    41–43, 45; healthcare **17**, 19–20;
    independence 45; population 5, **8**;
    right to shelter law 72
Indian Certificate of Secondary
    Education (ICSE) Board 37
inequality: as natural 1, 7
infant mortality 1, 60; infant mortality
    rate (IMR) 19, 60
innovation 1, 27, 43
international: assistance 5, 19, 75;
    human rights 38, 18, 40, 70, 71;
    initiatives 51; security 49 (*see
    also* food security); students/
    student education 34, 38; trade 37,
    50, 78, 80 (*see also* food trade)
International Fund for Agricultural
    Development (IFAD) 7, 51, 53,
    76, 78
International Journal of Housing Policy
    8, 14
International Monetary Fund (IMF) 48,
    76, 78, 79
International Parliament Union (IPU)
    45–46, 47
internet access 33, 35, 38
IPU *see* International Parliament Union

Japan: advanced education 28, **29**, 44;
    food security 50; gender bias
    41, **42–43**; healthcare 16, **17**,
    19, 21–23; population **5**; school
    system 34–35, **36**, 38
Japan Council for Quality Health Care
    (JQ) 22

Japan Health System Review 22, 27, 57
jobs 4, 7, 30, 61
JQ *see* Japan Council for Quality Health
    Care
justice 3

Lalueza-Fox, Carles 7
land rights 4, 73
language preservation 37
Law on Vocational Education 34
life expectancy (LE) 1, 16, 22–23, 60,
    63, **85–86**

malaria 25
maternal mortality ratio (MMR) 19,
    23–24, 60, 63
Menzingen verification experiment 49
migrants 4, 7
migration 4, 65, 72, 78, 80
Ministry of Housing and Urban Poverty
    Alleviation 72–73
MIT (Massachusetts Institute of
    Technology) 3
moral education 33

National Institute of Open Schooling
    (NIOS) 37
National Urban Housing and Habitat
    Policy (India) 72–73
National Urban Housing and Habitat
    Policy 2007 72–73
New Delhi 11–12
nuclear weapons 49

OECD *see* Organisation for Economic
    Co-operation and Development
Office of the High Commissioner for
    Human Rights (OHCHR)
    18, 70
OHCHR *see* Office of the High
    Commissioner for Human Rights
opportunities 4, 20, 38, 62–63
Organisation for Economic Co-operation
    and Development (OECD) 34

pandemic *see* COVID-19
peace 3, 38, 49, 53, 55
Philippines: advanced education 29, **30**,
    44; gender bias 43
PMAY *see* Pradhan Mantri Awas Yojana

policy 2, 3, 4, 8, 13, 14, 15; policy
    initiatives 2–5, 12, 16; policy
    makers 53, 54
Porter, Michael 3
poverty 2, 3, 4, 19, 61, 75; alleviation 72,
    73; eradication 25; line 14; rate
    67–68, **68**; reduction 2–3, 25,
    51, 59, 68, 72, 75–76
Pradhan Mantri Awas Yojana (PMAY)
    72–73
prejudice 4
private schools 5, 32, 35–36, 38, 52
Programme for International Student
    Assessment (PISA) 29, **30**, 31
Public: housing 8, 13; insurance 20;
    trends 23; underfunding 24
public policy 2

race 2, 62; *see also* ethnicity
research 1, 15, 21, 26, 27, 38, 39, 40, 43,
    49, 53, 56, 58, 65, 77, 80
resilience 4, 39, 56, 75
Rodrik, Dani 3, 6
Russia: education **29–31**, **36**; food
    security **50**; gender bias **41**;
    healthcare **17**, **83–84**; income
    inequality **66**, 67; population **5**;
    women empowerment **42**, 44

Scheidel, Walter 2
school: education 28, 32–33, 35; private
    5, 32, 35–36, **36**, 38, 52; public
    33; secondary 30, **31**, 33–35,
    36, 43, 63; vocational 34
Schwartz, Alex 8, 14
SDGs *see* Sustainable Development
    Goals
secondary school 30, **31**, 33–35, **36**,
    43, 63
segregation 8
sexual: harassment 62; orientation 63;
    reproductive health 25; violence
    47, 49, 62–63
Singapore 13, **67**, **85**
slums 7, **8**, 71, 72–73
Social and Economic Indicators 60
social progress 3–4, 62
Social Progress Index (SPI) 3, 17, 62, 64
socialism 68
Special Rapporteur (SR) 18, 26, 70, 71
SPI *see* Social Progress Index
SR *see* Special Rapporteur
Stanford University 2, 27

Statistical Annex 12, 16, 23, 26, 42, 50, 82
Stern, Scott 3
Sustainable Development Goals (SDGs) 3, 18, 24–25, 38, 47, 51–52, 57, 59, 71, 81

taxation 3, 19, 65
TB *see* tuberculosis
technology 4, 22, 27, 33, 36–37, 39, 57, 63, 77, 80, 81
tools 3, 33
transparent 18, 73
transport 1, 4, 37
transportation 53, 63
trends 2, 4; *see also* cross-country trends; public health
tuberculosis (TB) 16, **17**, 25, **83**

UHC *see* Universal Health Coverage
UN *see* United Nations
UN-Habitat 53, 75, 78–79
UNDP *see* United Nations Development Programme
UNESCO *see* United Nations Education, Scientific and Cultural Organization
UNICEF *see* United Nations Children's Fund
UNIDIR *see* United Nations Institute for Disarmament Research
United Nations (UN) 3, 6, 15, 25, 27, 46, 47, 48, 51–52, 59, 60, 70, 71, 75–80
United Nations Children's Fund (UNICEF) 35, 75, 78–79
United Nations Development Programme (UNDP) 41, 75, 78–79
United Nations Educational, Scientific and Cultural Organization (UNESCO) 35–36, 38, 53, 76, 79
United Nations Framework Convention of Climate Change (UNFCCC) 48, 78, 80
United Nations General Assembly 18, 40, 48–49, 52, 59, 70–71
United Nations Institute for Disarmament Research (UNIDIR) 49, 77–78, 80
United Nations reform 49
United Nations system (UN) 48–50, 77, 80

United Nations Universal Declaration of Human Rights 40, 70
United States: education 29–**31**, **36**; ethnicity 14; food security 50; gender bias 41; healthcare 16, **17**, 23–24; women empowerment 41, **42–43**, 44; women in politics 46
unity 37
Universal Health Coverage (UHC) 18–19
urban poor 72–73

vaccines 2, 16, 25
violence 41, 46, 63
visible equality 3, 5, 9–10, 13–14, 38, 52, 61–62
visible inequality 2–5, 10, 12, 32, 52, 60; *see also* housing

Washington DC 3, 9, 76, 77, 78, 79
water and sanitation 7, 12, **13**, 16, 18, 59–60, 62–63, **82**
wealth inequality 1–2, 4, 7, 10, 15, 40, 64–65, **66**
WEI *see* Women Empowerment Index
Westview Press 2, 6
WFP *see* World Food Programme
WHO *see* World Health Organization
WIR *see* World Inequality Lab
women: education and 28–29, **30**, 43–44, **44**, 45, 60; gender gaps 41–43, 53; mortality rate 19, 23–24, 60, 63; in politics **44–45**, 45–46, 61, 86; roles of 40
women empowerment 5, 40–41, 43, 46
Women Empowerment Index (WEI) 41, **42**
World Bank 3, 5, 48, 51, 60, 75, 77–79
World Development Indicators 61, 82
World Economic Forum 42–43, **86**
World Food Programme (WFP) 51, 76, 78–79
World Health Organization (WHO) 19, 22, 26, 53, 76, 78–80
World Inequality Lab (WIR) 2, 68
world population **5**, 51
World Social Report (WSR) 2020 4
WSR *see* World Social Report

Printed in the United States
by Baker & Taylor Publisher Services